THE TALE OF THEBES

THE TALE OF THEBES

ROGER LANCELYN GREEN

Illustrated by Jael Jordan

Cambridge University Press

CAMBRIDGE

LONDON · NEW YORK · MELBOURNE

Published by the Syndics of the Cambridge University Press
The Pitt Building, Trumpington Street, Cambridge CB2 1RP
Bentley House, 200 Euston Road, London NW1 2DB
32 East 57th Street, New York, NY 10022, USA
296 Beaconsfield Parade, Middle Park, Melbourne 3206, Australia

First published 1977

Printed in Great Britain at the
University Press, Cambridge

Library of Congress Cataloguing in Publication Data

Green, Roger Lancelyn.

The tale of Thebes.

SUMMARY: The stories of Cadmus, Dionysus, Oedipus, Antigone, and others collectively present the mythology associated with Thebes, some of the most famous of the Greek classical myths.

1. Mythology, Greek – Juvenile literature.
[1. Mythology, Greek] I. Title.

PZ8.1.G77Taj 292'.1'3 [398.2] 76-22979
ISBN 0 521 21410 6
ISBN 0 521 21411 4 pbk.

To

MARIA LIVADA

who helped me to see so much of

Greece

and so many Greek plays

CONTENTS

INTRODUCTION

And hast thou walked about – how strange a story –
In Thebes's streets three thousand years ago?

Not quite – but before writing this strange story of Thebes, I have walked about the streets of the modern city and found most of the ancient sites, just as I have visited every other place that comes into the story, except Psophis. And, because so many of the readers of this book are likely to visit Greece and see some at least of this most beautiful country, I have not hesitated to put in every place that is mentioned in the old Greek writings, often with a brief description of the scene.

In this I am following the example of the ancient Greeks themselves. However improbable the myth, however much embroidered by fancy the legend the poet or dramatist was telling, he always gave it 'a local habitation and a name'. For Greece is a small country, and the chances were, even then, that his hearers might well visit the place in question – be it Delphi or Dodona to consult the Oracles, or in peace or war Athens or Sparta, Thebes or Argos.

One of the delights in modern Hellenic travel is that most towns and villages have kept their ancient names and are still usually on or near the same spot as when Homer or Pindar, Æschylus, Sophocles or Euripides, Herodotus or Pausanias told of them – even such tiny places as Coroneia or Daulis, Orchomenos or Sicyon.

Besides the names of the places where the legendary events occurred, the Greeks delighted in giving and hearing full details of the names and relationships of all the characters concerned. As this is so much a part of the Greek tradition, I have not tried very hard to cut down on the names: but I could have put in a great many more. Not only does Apollodorus give a full list of the sons and daughters of Niobe who were killed before they had done anything, but he even names all Actaeon's dogs and Adrastus's horses!

To tell the Tale of Thebes has been a very different task from telling of Troy or the misfortunes of Agamemnon's family or the wanderings of Odysseus. It is a chronicle rather than a story, a collection of tales that join one on to another with only the thin golden thread of their Theban setting to hold them together – like the Necklace of Harmonia, which goes some way to giving it the same sort of unity that the Ring of the Nibelungs does to the Norse story of Sigurd.

But the 'matter of Thebes' has proved as rich or richer than the 'matter of Troy' in supplying great stories for the poets and tragedians. We have no Theban *Iliad* – though there was a *Thebaid*, now lost, which was thought to have been composed by Homer himself: 'With the exception of the *Iliad* and *Odyssey* I rate the *Thebaid* more highly than any other poem', wrote Pausanias, the author of the first traveller's guide to Greece, about A.D. 175 – and its loss is greatly to be regretted.

The only full-length epic we have about Thebes is one written in Latin by the Roman poet Statius about a hundred years before Pausanias. He tells only of the war of the Seven against Thebes, and puffs it all out to an intolerable length in a desperately florid and inflated style – in bad imitation of Vergil's *Aeneid*.

But if we have no Greek epic of Thebes, we have more and even finer tragedies than those about 'Pelops' line, or the tale of 'Troy divine'. Æschylus, the earliest of the extant dramatists, has left us *The Seven Against Thebes*, a play about the strife between Eteocles and Polynices. But it was Sophocles, the second great dramatist, who has given us the most glorious works about Thebes – *Oedipus the King*, one of the world's greatest plays, *Oedipus at Colonus* and *Antigone*; and Euripides runs him a close second with *The Bacchae*, *The Phoenician Women* (Eteocles and Polynices and the Seven) and *The Suppliants* (the burial of the Seven).

All of these plays have been used in my retelling, and have supplied many passages of dialogue as well. The next most important source has been the late Greek epic, *The Dionysiaca* of Nonnos of Panopolis in Egypt, written about A.D. 500, and historians and mythographers such as Apollodorus and Diodorus of Sicily. But I have ransacked Greek and Latin literature for scraps of narrative or dialogue – jumping from Homer and Theocritus and Bion to Ovid and Horace, Pausanias and Antoninus Liberalis to Parthenius and

Hyginus. A detailed list would be out of place, but I can assure the reader that everything in this book has full classical authority and that my only departures from my originals have been to cast a few passages into dialogue form and add a few descriptions of scenes and places. Where authorities differed, I have used that which fitted best into the general scheme. But usually I have tried to combine versions as far as possible. For example, Sophocles in his *Oedipus the King* says that Jocasta hanged herself, and was dead before Oedipus went into exile; but Euripides in his *Phoenician Women* brings her on stage still alive some years later when the Seven launched their attack on Thebes. So as not to depart too far from the better known version which Sophocles gives, I have suggested that she did hang herself – but was cut down in time, before she was completely strangled.

And now, like Pindar the great Theban poet: 'I come from splendid Thebes, and I bring a song that tells of mighty deeds . . .'

ROGER LANCELYN GREEN

Map 1. The whole Greek World

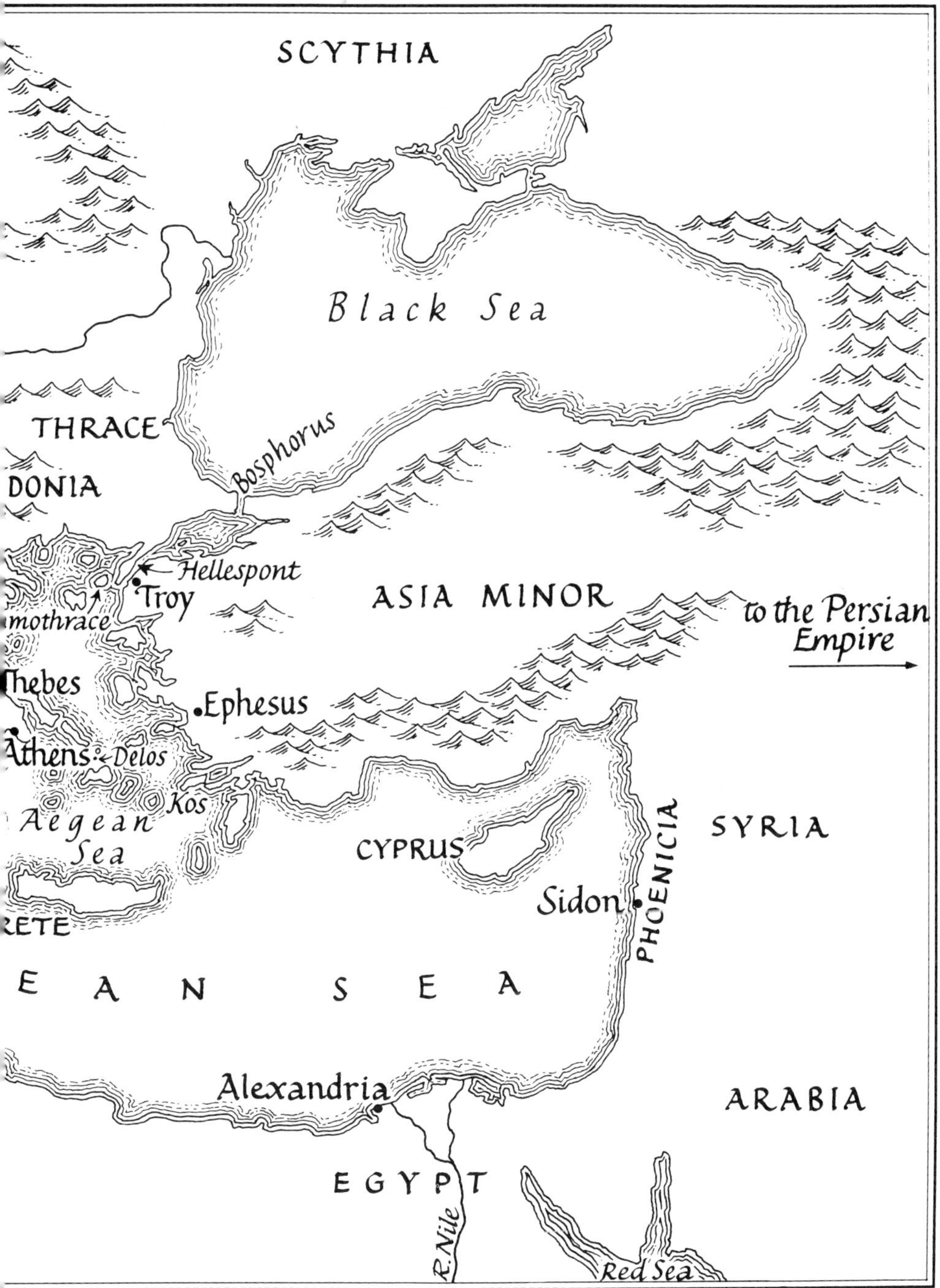
SCYTHIA
Black Sea
THRACE
DONIA
Bosphorus
Hellespont
Troy
mothrace
ASIA MINOR
to the Persian Empire
Thebes
Ephesus
Athens
Delos
Kos
Aegean Sea
CYPRUS
SYRIA
PHOENICIA
Sidon
RETE
EAN SEA
Alexandria
ARABIA
EGYPT
R. Nile
Red Sea

Mt. Oeta
Trachis
Thermopylae
OPUNTIA
Drymaea
Tithorea
R. Cephisus
PHOCIS
Mt. Parnassus
Amphissa
Daulis
Delphi
Crisaean Plain
CLEFT WAY
Cirrha
Orchomenus
Copae
Panopeus
Lebadea
Lake Copais
Coronea
Haliartus
Mt. Helicon
Thisbe
Corinthian
Gulf
Mt. Ceranea
Sicyon
PELOPONNESUS
THE ISTHMUS
SCIRONIAN WAY
Corinth

Map 2. Central Greece

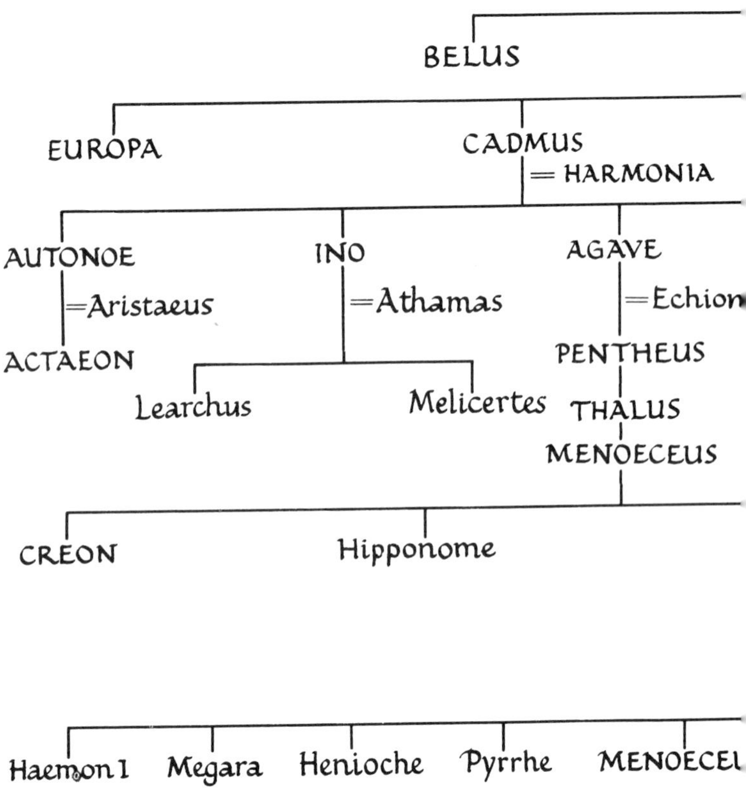

The Royal Family of Thebes

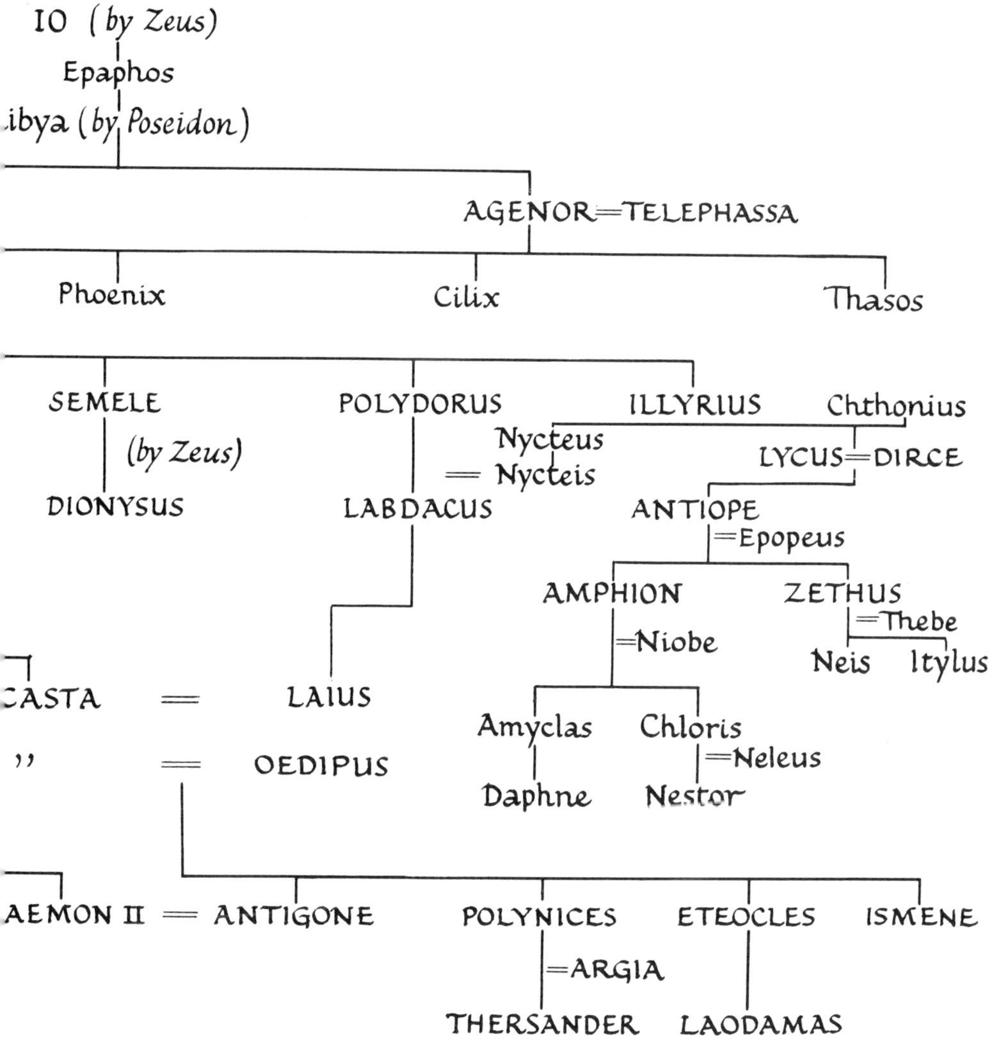
IO (by Zeus)
Epaphos
ibya (by Poseidon)
AGENOR = TELEPHASSA
Phoenix
Cilix
Thasos
SEMELE
(by Zeus)
DIONYSUS
POLYDORUS
= Nycteis
LABDACUS
ILLYRIUS
Nycteus
Chthonius
LYCUS = DIRCE
ANTIOPE
= Epopeus
AMPHION
= Niobe
ZETHUS
= Thebe
Neis
Itylus
Amyclas
Daphne
Chloris
= Neleus
Nestor
CASTA = LAIUS
" = OEDIPUS
AEMON II = ANTIGONE
POLYNICES
= ARGIA
THERSANDER
ETEOCLES
LAODAMAS
ISMENE

I

THE STORY OF IO

In the misty morning of the world, when the gods of Olympus still mingled freely with the sons and daughters of men, and Zeus, the King of the Gods, was dividing the fair land of Greece among those who were destined to become the ancestors of the Heroes who were to found its famous cities, there was a King of Argos called Inachus.

It may be that Inachus came sailing over the sea from distant Egypt, and settled at Argos; or it may be that, as legends told, he was the son of the Sea itself – of Ocean, the great river which was thought to flow round the whole world. But he became King of Argos, in the great fertile plain famous in after days for its horses and its olive-groves, the land whose chief city was soon to be Mycenae; and he married Argeria the princess whom he found there waiting for him, and they had several children.

Fairest among them was their daughter Io, who became the first priestess of Hera, Queen of Olympus, and tended her shrine near Mycenae, the Heraion, the ruins of which may still be seen on the hillside overlooking the great plain of Argolis.

Io grew up in this quiet and beautiful spot, happy to serve Hera and remain her virgin priestess all her life. But Zeus had other, greater plans for her; and when she was grown into womanhood terrible dreams began to haunt her night by night. These visions were strange and confused, for sometimes it seemed that a great voice spoke to her, saying: 'Royal maiden, you shall not go childless all your days, for Zeus himself shall be the father of your son – and your son shall be the ancestor of mighty kings. Therefore leave this shrine and go down to the meadows at Lerna beside the sea, to the rich pastures where your father's cattle graze.' But then the dream would become a nightmare in which Io saw herself changed into strange and terrifying forms and rushing over the earth seeking always to escape from some horror that pursued her.

At last she could endure no longer in silence, and sent for her father and told him all that she could remember of her dreams.

Inachus was deeply troubled, and it seemed best to him that he should consult the Oracles of the gods. So first he sent messengers to Delphi where Apollo had his Oracle, which was to become the most famous in all the ancient world. But from Delphi he got back only strange and riddling replies that told him nothing.

Then he sent messengers to Dodona in the north of Greece where Zeus had his temple by the Talking Oaktree with the leaves whose whisper told of things to come. And the priests of Zeus listened to the murmur of the leaves and told the messengers in plain terms that by the will of Zeus Io must leave the temple of Hera and go alone to wander in the meadows of Lerna near the mouth of the Haliacmon, the river of Argos.

At first Inachus refused to obey the words of the Oracle. But Zeus, as a sign that he must be obeyed, flung a thunderbolt which dried up the stream of the River Haliacmon – and dry it remains to this day except in early spring when the torrents come down from the melting snows on the mountains of Arcadia.

Then Inachus hesitated no longer. Sadly he led Io out of the Heraion and down across the plain to where the river had flowed into the sea near Lerna, beyond the hill of Argos. And there he left her to weep and lament her sad fate under the olive trees by the stony bed of the stream.

When Io was alone, Zeus cast a silver mist about himself and drew near to her. But Hera, who was jealous lest Zeus intended to make Io a goddess in Argolis instead of her, and angry that her priestess had been taken from the shrine, came down from Olympus in a chariot drawn by two peacocks – which at that time had tails of plain green and gold.

As she drew near, the magic mist faded away and Zeus stood waiting for her. But before the mist cleared, he touched Io on the head and she was transformed into a white heifer with golden horns.

Hera looked at the beautiful creature with admiration – but also with suspicion. For she knew that the mist could not have come by natural means on a summer's day when there was no drop of water in the River Haliacmon.

But she smiled sweetly upon Zeus, praised the beauty of the heifer – and begged it of him as a gift. And there was nothing Zeus could do but give the disguised Io to her, and retire to Olympus with the best grace he could – though muttering angrily to himself until the thunder rumbled threateningly over the mountains as he passed.

Triumphantly Hera led the white heifer across the plain to one of her sacred groves of olive trees in a deep valley below the hill on which Mycenae was soon to stand. There she tethered Io to a tree, and set her servant the monster Argus to guard her. Now this Argus had a hundred eyes all round his head so that it was impossible for anyone to steal up to him unseen; and as only two of his eyes were closed at one time when he slept, it was impossible to surprise him even then.

There for a long time poor Io dwelt in her alien form, eating the grass and lying down to chew the cud like other cows, but still able to think with her own mind and to grieve over her strange fate and wonder fearfully what was to become of her.

Zeus too was troubled, and he turned himself into a falcon and flew hither and thither among the olive trees of Argolis until at last he found the white heifer who was Io and her sleepless guardian. Not wishing to anger Hera by any direct action, Zeus returned to Olympus and bade his son Hermes the Messenger of the Gods go to the grove in Argolis and see if by any means he could kill Argus or put him to sleep, or persuade him to give up his charge. For Hermes was also the God of Thieves and the most cunning of all the Immortals.

Away sprang Hermes on his winged sandals and sped through the sky like a flash of light until he came to the Mountain of the Sun behind Mycenae. There he disguised himself as a mortal shepherd, and drove his flock of goats down the steep hillside and through the groves of trees until he came to the valley by the Choina stream where Argus sat on a rock guarding Io who was looking at her reflection in a pool and weeping great tears to see the white cow's face with its horns above reflected instead of her own.

'Greetings, herdsman!' called Hermes as he came within sight of Argus. 'Can you tell me where I can find good grazing for my goats?'

'There is no richer grass in all Argolis than hereabouts', answered Argus. 'And here too you may find fine trees under which you or any other shepherd may shelter from the sun. So come and sit by me on this rock, for I grow lonely.'

So Hermes came and sat by Argus and told him many merry tales. Then he took out his pipes made of reeds and began to play soft, sleepy tunes on them. But Argus strove valiantly against the urge to sleep, although many of his eyes began to close, and presently he said, in his efforts to keep awake:

'Tell me, stranger, what is that wonderful thing on which you play such sweet tunes? For I have never until now seen or heard anything like it.'

Then, playing still more softly and dreamily, and pausing between tunes to tell his story in low, languorous tones, Hermes told how his pipes had been made. He told of the nymph called Syrinx whom the goat-footed god Pan fell in love with as she wandered over the hills of Arcadia away to the west of Argolis; how Pan pursued her and she ran and ran until she came to the River Ladon which checked her flight; how she prayed to the God of the River to help her, and how as Pan triumphantly clasped her in his arms she was turned into a bundle of reeds. He told how Pan uttered a great sigh of disappointment, and how the reeds were stirred so tunefully that Pan was inspired to cut them and join them together with wax and make the first Pan-pipes, which were called syrinx after the nymph . . .

And Hermes paused, for every one of the hundred eyes of Argus was closed in sleep by the dreamy music and the soothing words of the story. Swiftly and silently Hermes drew his sharp sword and cut off Argus's head with one blow. Then he turned to where Io the white heifer was tethered, loosed the halter from her neck, and began to lead her away through the olive groves.

But Hera was told swiftly by her own messenger the cuckoo of what had happened. In a whirlwind of anger she came lashing across the olive trees of Argolis and found Argus dead. Then she took his hundred eyes and set them in her peacocks' tails, where they shine to this day. And she sent a fierce gadfly to pursue Io and to sting her whenever it caught up with her.

Maddened by the pain, Io still in the form of a heifer fled away and away across the world. First she went westward over the mountains and through the valleys of Arcadia until she came to the

Jael Jordan

sea. Into it she plunged and swam north past the islands of Cephallonia and Ithaca, past Leucas and Paxos and Corcyra, which is now called Corfu: and the waters through which she swam have been called after her the Ionian Sea to this very day.

Then Io came to the shore of Illyria and fled across the north of Greece, ever pursued and tormented by the gadfly. Through Macedonia and Thrace she went until she came to the narrow strait which separates Europe from Asia, near where the city of Constantinople was to stand in after days. Across this she swam – and it has ever since been called the Bosphorus, which means the Ox Ford.

On and on went Io from land to land, through Asia Minor and Palestine, until at last she came to Egypt. There she fell down, utterly exhausted, by the banks of the Nile, and raising her head she prayed to Zeus in words of grief, which sounded like the wild blarting of a cow in pain, begging for release or death.

And Zeus, to whom all this was but part of the great plan which he alone could see – though even he could not see all of it – turned now to Hera and said:

'Fear no more for the future of Argos, nor for your honour there. I have no thought in my mind of taking away the smallest part of your worship as the great Goddess of Argolis. Though Io's descendants shall be its kings, Perseus and Heracles, it shall never cease to be your land, nor the Argives your people. For I have a greater destiny still in store for others of Io's descendants. They shall be kings of Crete; they shall be kings of Cilicia and Thasos; but, above all, one of them shall found the great city of seven-gated Thebes, which shall be among the most famous in all Greece. Yes, by Styx I swear that after your city of Mycenae that is just coming to birth, and Athens which is not yet born, Thebes shall be numbered with the great cities of all time.'

Then Hera's wrath was wiped away; and by her will Io was changed into what she had been. The rough hair fell away from her body; her horns disappeared; her great, mad eyes grew smaller; her hooves faded away, and she stood once more upon her feet, the loveliest maiden on all the earth.

And when Io had cast off her cowlike form, Zeus stretched out his hand and touched her on the forehead. And presently she bore a son whose name was Epaphos. He became a king of Egypt, marrying the princess Memphis, only child of the Pharaoh of that day; and from his daughter Libya – who founded the great country in North Africa which took her name – was born Belus, next Pharaoh of Egypt, and Agenor who was later to be King of Phoenicia.

But back in Argos, King Inachus grieved so much over the loss of his daughter that at length he went mad and flung himself into the River Haliacmon when it was in flood after the winter snows had melted in Arcadia. And his son Phroneus ruled in his stead; and in memory of his father he changed the name of the river of Argos from Haliacmon to Inachus, by which name it is known to this day.

II

THE QUEST FOR EUROPA

When Belus, the descendant of Io, became ruler of Egypt, his younger brother Agenor set out to seek his fortune, and in time he came to the city of Sidon in the country that was later to be called Palestine. There he married the princess Telephassa, and the two of them ruled peaceably over Sidon and the land round about it, and had four sons and a daughter called Europa.

Both Agenor and Telephassa loved her above all their children – and she was exceedingly beautiful, even as if she had been one of the Immortals who dwelt on Olympus. And indeed Zeus, the King of Gods and Men, had given her beauty and had laid his plans carefully so that she should give her name to the continent of Europe and found a great race of kings in the island of Crete. And other things too were decreed by Zeus that would be brought about because of Europa's beauty and the love which her parents and her four brothers bore her.

When the time was ripe Zeus sent strange dreams to Europa which caused her one bright spring morning to gather together her company of girls, all born in the same year that she was and her dearest friends, and set off with them to gather flowers in the meadows beside the sea.

It was a perfect spring day, and the earth was carpeted with flowers. Europa and her companions began to gather them into their baskets – one girl plucking the sweet-scented narcissus, another the hyacinth, another the violet and a fourth the creeping thyme. Europa's closest friend was gathering the fragrant tresses of the yellow crocus, but she herself found out the first wild roses, shining among the other flowers like Aphrodite the Goddess of Beauty among her nymphs.

When they were all happily engaged, Zeus took upon himself the shape of a bull – a beautiful white bull with golden horns, even as the heifer into which he had once turned Europa's ancestress Io.

Like Io, this bull was quite unlike those which pull the plough or draw the loaded carts. Far from frightened, Europa and her companions all felt a great desire to run up and stroke this bull who came and breathed his sweet-smelling breath on Europa's feet and cast a glamour over her so that at length she flung her arms round his neck and kissed him on the forehead. Then she and the rest made garlands of flowers which they hung about the bull; and presently, much daring, Europa climbed upon his back and sat upon his great arched neck, holding the golden horns with both hands.

'Come along!' she called to her friends. 'Climb up behind me! There's room for all of us, and this bull is so tame and gentle that he will do us no harm!'

But even as they drew near to do as she suggested, the bull suddenly sprang up with Europa alone on his back and set off towards the sea at top speed. Europa screamed with fright, and called to her friends to help her. But in vain: they could not keep up with the bull, and she dared not try to jump from its back as it was going so fast.

The bull did not stop when he got to the shore, but went straight into the sea, or onto it as it seemed, for the waves grew smooth beneath his hooves, and he sped forward without wetting even Europa's feet, as she sat on his broad shoulders clinging to the golden horns.

They went so fast that the land was soon out of sight, and presently Europa plucked up enough courage to speak to her strange steed, saying timidly:

'Bull-god, where are you taking me? What are you? How are you able to speed across the sea as if it were a meadow? Bulls do not dwell in the sea, any more than dolphins do on land: but land and sea seem to be as one to you. Bull-god, pity me, and take me back to my home, to my father and mother, and to my four brothers who love me so dearly.'

Then the bull answered her gently: 'Take courage, maiden, and have no fear of the deep sea, or of me carrying you over it. For know that, though I wear the form of a bull, I am Zeus: for I can take on whatever shape I will. Weep no more, for this is your wedding day, and in Crete where I was born I shall be your husband, and

Jael Jordan

you shall bear children who shall be great and famous to all time: Minos, father to a line of kings who shall rule over Crete; and Rhadamanthys who shall be the justest of all men, and, when his long life on earth is ended, shall be judge among the dead in the kingdom of my brother Hades.'

As Zeus spoke a great awe and rapture came over Europa so that she was no more afraid. And she marvelled when out of the sea rose a company of Nereids, sea-nymphs, riding on dolphins, their green hair falling over their naked shoulders; and when other half-divine creatures of the sea came to join them – the Tritons or mermen, blowing a bridal hymn on their conches; and when Poseidon the God of the Sea, with Amphitrite his Queen, came to do honour to this strange wedding of his brother Zeus.

And when they came at length to the beautiful island of Crete, Aphrodite, Goddess of Love, was waiting to join their hands as Zeus stepped ashore and in an instant took on his own form again. And she led them up the long valleys and through the scented fir trees of Mount Ida to the Cave of Dicte, their wedding bower.

But at Sidon King Agenor knew nothing of what had befallen his daughter; and when her frightened companions had come rushing to the palace and told him and Queen Telephassa of the magic bull which had come and carried Europa away over the sea, his rage and grief knew no bounds. In despair bordering on madness he sent for his sons Phoenix, Cadmus, Cilix and Thasus, and cried out:

'Your sister Europa has been stolen away and carried over the sea by some evil wizard in the form of a bull. Set out, all four of you, in search of her: and do not any of you dare to return without her. I will slay whoever does with my own hand!'

So the four princes set forth on their quest. Phoenix went south and west, into Egypt and Libya and along all the coast of North Africa. But he could find no trace of Europa; and at length, hearing that his father had died, he returned to Sidon and became king not only of the city but of all the country round about, which henceforth was known as Phoenicia after him.

Cilix went east and north into Asia Minor and searched through all the country that is now called Turkey. But not finding Europa, and afraid to return home, he and his followers settled in that part of the country which became known as Cilicia after him.

Cadmus, however, gathered many men together and set sail with a small fleet of ships. And both Telephassa his mother and his brother Thasus went with him. And first of all they came to the island of Thera, which is now called Santorin by some people. They did not find Europa there, but one ship gave up the search and the sailors in it settled on that island. And then, driven off their course by the will of Zeus, instead of going south to Crete, they went to the east and landed on the island of Rhodes. And there two ships stayed behind and their crews settled in that land of peace and beauty.

But Cadmus and the rest of his fleet sailed to the north and came at length to another island off the coast of Thrace where Thasus decided to remain with the company of his ship; and that island is called Thasos after him to this day.

Cadmus, however, sailed over to the mainland of Thrace with such ships as remained to him; and there he stayed for more than a year. For his mother Telephassa was taken ill and could go no further; and there at length she died and was buried.

After this his men wished to remain and settle where they were. But Cadmus felt sure that he was intended for something better than to settle in this drear northern land. And so he let his men remain in Thrace and rest after their wanderings for one year while he set out alone to see where the gods would lead him – for suddenly he felt as if he were called away to perform some great task. And his men were only too willing to rest themselves among the kindly and hospitable men of Thrace.

But Cadmus set off by himself and wandered away into the unexplored country to the north of Thrace, on the edge of the wild desert where strange savage creatures dwelt; where the wild tribes of the one-eyed Animaspi hunted for the gold which the winged griffins hid among the rocks and the dragons guarded in their deep caves beneath the mountains.

And there Cadmus found himself playing a part in events so strange that they seemed like a dream of some other, earlier world. For suddenly as he wandered on the heights of Mount Haemus, Hermes the Messenger of Zeus met him.

'Do not be afraid, Cadmus son of Agenor', said Hermes. 'Zeus himself has need of your aid, and for this reason have you been drawn hither away from all your companions. Be brave and daring now, and Zeus will reward you with an Immortal bride and make you the founder of a great and famous city far away in the land of Greece.'

Then Hermes began to tell Cadmus strange things. He told of the wars which Zeus and the Gods of Olympus had been forced to wage against the Titans, the old monstrous gods of earlier days, and of how that war had been won when Zeus was able to cast them down into Tartarus, the flaming prison under the earth, with the aid of the thunderbolts that the Cyclops forged for him on the island of Lemnos.

'These Titans were the children of Earth', Hermes told him. 'And Earth has now brought forth yet another Titan – a Giant called Typhon – whom she hid away in a cave of the mountains until he could take Zeus by surprise. And this he did when Zeus had laid aside his thunderbolts and was resting on a hillside not far from here. And the Giant overcame Zeus for long enough to cut away the sinews of his hands and feet with a magic sickle of adamant which had belonged to Cronos the King of the Titans. Now Zeus lies helpless, unable to return to Olympus or to hurl his thunderbolts. But Typhon was sorely wounded also, and he rests in his cave not far from here until he has recovered his strength; and then he plans to set the Titans free and imprison us who dwell on Olympus in Tartarus in their stead.

'So we must recover the sinews of Zeus from Typhon by guile – for force cannot prevail against so mighty a Giant until Zeus can once more wield his thunderbolts and drive his chariot across the sky. And, being himself an Immortal, Typhon would recognise even me, however cleverly I was disguised, if I came near him. But you he would not suspect: and if you will do exactly as I tell you, there will be no difficulty in deceiving him – for, in spite of their size and strength, Giants are inclined to be stupid.'

At first Cadmus was very much afraid. But he was young and brave and adventurous; and soon he was listening eagerly to the plan which Hermes had made, and beginning to fit himself for carrying it out.

For Hermes led him over the mountainside and through the forest to an open glade as near the Giant's cave as they dared. And then out of the forest came merry Pan, the goat-footed god of flocks and herds and of all wild things: and Pan brought with him a flock of sheep and the garments and crook of a shepherd with which he disguised Cadmus. Next Pan and Hermes helped him to build a hut of mats of wattled reeds fixed on stakes driven into the ground: and Hermes placed in the hut all things needful, while Pan took his own syrinx, his reed-pipes, and taught Cadmus how to play on them.

'Now Cadmus!' laughed Pan. 'Play the pipes and herd your sheep – and there shall be fine weather in heaven once again!'

Then the two gods left him, and Cadmus sat himself down under a shady tree and began to play long and loud upon the pipes while the sheep grazed lazily about him or slept in the drowsy summer weather.

Presently Typhon the Giant awoke from his afternoon slumbers and heard the sweet sound of the syrinx. He loved music and was enchanted by what he heard. Slowly he rose to his feet and strode through the trees which barely came up to his waist until he came to the glade where Cadmus sat.

When he saw the Giant coming towards him Cadmus sprang to his feet in terror and seemed about to run away – only his fear rooted him to the ground.

'Do not be afraid, shepherd!' boomed Typhon. 'You need not run away from me. I would think it shame to pursue a mere mortal man – I who have chased Zeus himself, yes, and caught him too! A fine feat indeed it would be to steal your pipes, after I have stolen the very thunderbolts of Zeus! Keep your pipes – and play on them for me to make me happy, and I'll give you kingdoms for your reward when I have conquered the whole world!'

So Cadmus played the most bewitching tune he knew: and indeed the pipes themselves seemed to be inspired as if Pan himself were playing them – or as if the spirit of the nymph Syrinx still dwelt in them.

But when he had finished the tune and saw that Typhon was already caught in the web of fate, he smiled at the Giant and uttered artful words:

'You like the little tune of my pipes? What then would you do if I played you a hymn of victory on the seven-stringed lyre? For I can play better even than Apollo himself – and indeed I played a match with him and beat him so surely that Zeus burnt to dust the fine strings of my lyre to please his defeated son. But if ever again I can find sinews with which to string my lyre, I'll show you what music really is. I'll play a tune that will bewitch the trees and the mountains, that will tame the wild beasts and make them follow me wherever I go – that will make the sea itself stand still to listen. But alas, my lyre is broken and the only music I can make is with these simple pipes such as shepherds use.'

When Typhon heard this he was completely beguiled. 'Wait!' he rumbled; and with a few steps he had returned to his cave and come back again with the sinews which he had torn from the hands and feet of Zeus. These he flung to Cadmus, who bowed his thanks, took up the broken lyre which he had ready, and retired into his hut as if to mend it with the sinews which the Giant had given to him.

And presently indeed there came from within the hut music of the lyre so sweet that any but Typhon would have known that only Apollo himself, the God of Music, could have been playing.

But meanwhile Cadmus crept away behind the hut into the thickest part of the wood where Hermes was waiting for him. Swiftly Hermes carried the sinews to Zeus, while Cadmus fled away down towards the plain of Thrace where his men and ships were waiting for him.

As soon as all was well the music ceased, and a low mutter of thunder told the startled Giant that Zeus was not only whole once more but had recaptured the thunderbolts which had been hidden in the cave where the sinews had lain.

After that there was no escape for Typhon, who fled across the earth until he came to the south of Italy where Zeus caught up with him, laid him low with a thunderbolt, and imprisoned him for ever under Mount Etna – where he still breathes smoke and fire through the crater of the volcano.

But Cadmus and his followers sailed away over smooth seas with gentle breezes to waft them on their way. And very soon they came to the mysterious island of Samothrace where they anchored at the entrance to a valley which runs up to the foot of the mighty mountain with its head hidden in the clouds which takes up most of the island.

III

CADMUS AND HARMONIA

Cadmus anchored with his ships in the harbour at Samothrace late in the evening, and early next morning he set out alone to see who dwelt there and why Zeus had brought him to this mysterious island.

Up the valley he went beside a stream which sparkled in the early spring sunlight in a series of little waterfalls and rapids. On his right a low ridge stretched up before him to join the foothills of the great mountain, and on his left he saw a far higher and steeper spur of the mountain on which he soon made out the mighty walls of a great citadel built of gigantic stones fitted cunningly together.

Soon the valley opened out in front of him into a wide glade with a temple and gardens and behind them other buildings and a winding road up to the citadel. People were moving about at a distance, and Cadmus was about to approach and speak to some of them, when he suddenly found that a tall and stately woman was walking beside him, carrying on her arm a great silver jug full of water from the Fountain of Victory which gushed out on the hillside to his right. At once she began:

'Prince Cadmus, I am sent to lead you to King Emathion and his mother Queen Electra who await you in the palace. For Hermes the Messenger has been to visit them with the commands of Zeus; and I, Peitho, the hand-maiden of Aphrodite, Goddess of Love, am sent to lead you to them unseen of any. For know that with them dwells Harmonia, the daughter of Aphrodite and of Ares, the God of War – and that she is destined to be your bride. She will be the first Queen of the city you are to found far away in Greece, which will one day be called Thebes of the Seven Gates. Although she is a daughter of two Immortals, Harmonia had been brought up since she was born by Queen Electra, who is herself half divine, being the daughter of Atlas the Titan and of Pleione the daughter of Ocean. Queen Electra's elder son is Dardanus, whose father is said to be Zeus himself; but Dardanus has gone across the sea to the land of Troy to found there the great city of Ilion, and his brother Emathion rules here in Samothrace in his stead. Come with me to where he awaits you – and as we go I will tell you a merry tale of how Ares and Aphrodite became the parents of Harmonia.'

So Peitho led Cadmus through the city, hidden by a silver mist of the morning so that no one saw them as they passed. And as they went Peitho told him the tale of how Aphrodite the Love-Goddess, who overcomes all by her powers was herself overcome by love. For she was wedded to Hephaestus, the lame and ugly God of Craftsmen, the smith of the gods who had his forge under the volcanic island of Lemnos where the one-eyed giants, the Cyclopes, worked for him making the thunderbolts for Zeus. Aphrodite had little love for Hephaestus, and very soon she fell in love with Ares, the War-God, strong and handsome. Whenever Hephaestus was away from Olympus, attending to his forge on Lemnos, Ares would visit Aphrodite secretly, and none of the Immortals knew of their intrigue – save one alone, Helios who drives the chariot of the sun across the sky each day. And at last Helios told Hephaestus what was going on: but when Hephaestus spoke of his suspicions none of the Immortals would believe him.

So the Lame God thought of a cunning scheme. He went off to Lemnos and prepared a snare of woven gold and strong, subtle springs; and this he hung secretly among the shadowy roof-beams above the great golden bed in his palace on Olympus, and set the delicate trap with its hair-trigger. Then he let it be known that he must go away to Lemnos for a long spell of work, and the Immortals saw him depart, and both Ares and Aphrodite were there to see him on his way. But he did not go far; and very soon had stolen back secretly to Olympus.

Meanwhile, suspecting nothing of the Lame God's wiles, Ares slipped unseen into the palace of Hephaestus; and there Aphrodite was waiting for him – nor was the Goddess of Love less eager in their love-making than the God of War. But as soon as he held her close the subtle snare was released and the golden meshes fell about the guilty pair and the golden springs closed and held them immovable.

Then Hephaestus came out of his hiding place and entered the presence of Zeus and the other gods as they sat at the banquet board eating the ambrosia and drinking the nectar – the food and wine of the Immortals – and cried:

'Father Zeus, and you other blessed gods that live for ever, come with me and see a mirthful sight, and yet a cruel one: come and see how Aphrodite my fair wife has deceived me, scorning my lameness maybe, and has given herself in love to Ares the straight and strong of limb!'

So Hephaestus led the other Immortals to the great bed-chamber in his palace, and they saw how Ares and Aphrodite were held together there against their will – and laughter unquenchable rose among the blessed gods as they beheld the cunning snare in which the lovers were caught.

'And so', Peitho concluded her tale to Cadmus, 'Ares withdrew for a time from Olympus and dwells among men, where he stirs up many a savage war. But Aphrodite and Hephaestus were soon reconciled – for who can withstand Love Herself? Yet when Harmonia was born, Zeus decreed that she must be brought up among mortals; and he gave her to Queen Electra to bring up as her own daughter and the foster-sister of Emathion here in the golden palace on Samothrace and beneath the blossoming trees of its happy gardens.'

By now Peitho had brought Cadmus to the entrance of the palace, unseen by any, and here she left him and vanished from human sight.

But Cadmus stood marvelling at the shining beauty of the building, which Hephaestus had constructed for Electra when first she came to Samothrace as a bride, before the time when Harmonia was entrusted to her care. About and behind it on the hill-top towered a wall of gigantic hewn stones cunningly shaped and fitted together so that they would remain standing many thousands of years later. The palace itself was coated with plates of gold and bronze, decorated with painted columns and set with statues of dogs wrought from silver and from gold so life-like that they seemed ready to spring upon the unwary visitor: indeed more than once Cadmus nearly sat down upon the ground – a sign of friendship which Greek dogs recognise even to this day.

At length he came into the megaron, the great hall where a fire burnt always beneath the opening in the roof. There King Emathion sat on his golden throne to welcome his guest. And for a while Emathion spoke no word, so struck with amazement was he at the strength and beauty of this alien prince who came to visit him.

But soon he rose and extended both hands to the guest whom Zeus, the God of Guests had sent to him. And presently his mother, Queen Electra, herself like in beauty to the Immortal goddesses, came forth from the inner chamber to welcome him also, and the feast was set in the sacred halls of Samothrace.

And when the feast was ended came the dancers and musicians – the strange Initiates of the Mysteries of the Cabeiroi of Samothrace of which no one knows the truth even to this day – and they danced the sacred dances before Cadmus and performed the sacred celebration, so that the entertainment became also an act of worship.

After it was ended Cadmus told the tale of his adventures to Electra and Emathion – both of how he had set out from Sidon in search of Europa, and of the high service which Zeus himself had demanded of him.

And thereafter, having been already told by the divine messenger Hermes of what was destined, the fair Queen Electra led Cadmus into the secret garden of the palace now lit by the moon, and left him alone there until presently he saw Harmonia gliding in and out of the silver beams and the sable shadows – as fair as Selene the Moon-Goddess herself when she enchanted the mortal prince Endymion and cast him into his immortal sleep on Mount Latmos in the eastern land of Ionia.

And to Harmonia Cadmus seemed like one of the Immortal gods come down from Olympus to woo her: for so were all things brought about by Aphrodite her mother, the Immortal who sets sweet love and desire in the hearts of mortal men and women. Cadmus had no thought but of the loveliness of his bride-to-be; and Harmonia no desire other than to follow Cadmus wheresoever he should sail, leaving lovely Samothrace and making her home wherever his home should be.

So Electra and Emathion led the two into the round temple of the Mysteries and joined their hands in pledge of the wedding that was to be. But even as their hands were joined there came Hermes the Messenger and spoke the will of Zeus, saying:

'Set sail now over the deep sea to Delphi and learn from Apollo by his oracle beside the Spring of Castalia, where your city shall be. And when all is accomplished and you have built the fair citadel of Cadmeia, then – most blessed of mortals – the Immortal gods themselves shall come as guests to your wedding, in honour of what Cadmus did when the hour of great danger came upon Zeus himself.

'But until that day when the golden tables are set on the hill of Cadmeia above the springs of Dirce, which in after days shall be called Thebes of the Seven Gates, I charge you that you be no more to one another than brother and sister, until Harmonia kneels before the altar of her mother Aphrodite upon that wedding day which is to be.'

So with bowed heads they went their separate ways. But next morning Cadmus got ready his two stout ships and to them King Emathion added a third in which Harmonia and her attendants were to sail. Now the carved figure-head of this ship was shaped in the likeness of Heavenly Aphrodite, pure love free from all bodily desires. But of the two ships which Cadmus had brought with him one bore as figure-head laughter-loving Aphrodite as she first rose from the sea with no thought but of the Sweet Desire that she brings to all living creatures; and the other ship bore a likeness of Aphrodite also – but Aphrodite the Righteous who brings a curse and utter destruction upon all those who follow unlawful passions and unnatural lusts and would profane the mysteries of Heavenly Love and the innocent joys of Sweet Desire.

Then they bade farewell to Emathion and Electra, and Harmonia wept a little at parting from her adopted brother and foster-mother, and at leaving the enchanted island which had been her home since she could remember and where she had lived so happily amid so much peace and beauty.

But very soon she dried her tears and, as the towering mountain of Samothrace grew fainter and fainter in the mists behind her, she sat on the poop of her ship looking eagerly forward over the sparkling sea where the dolphins leapt and gambled and the halcyons 'the sea-blue birds of the spring' flitted over the waves.

Southward they went through the early summer weather with never a storm to trouble them, but always a steady breeze to carry them on their way. Past the islands of Lemnos and Skyros they went, between Andros and Euboea, and so round the southern shores of Greece – and even as they rounded Malea, the cape of storms, and left Cythera to the south, the gentle breezes did not desert them.

Then they turned north into the Ionian Sea, and the wind changed with their course and blew gently but strongly from the south, until they turned east once more and sailed up the narrow Gulf of Corinth between the towering mountains of Arcadia to the south and Aetolia to the north. And it seemed that the sea-nymphs guided their ships, for suddenly as the breeze fell they found themselves floating into the wide bay of Crissa on the north coast, and they needed scarcely to put out their oars to bring them to the little harbour of Cirrha (which today is called Itea) below the foot-hills of the mighty mountain of Parnassus.

In the morning the people of Cirrha came down to the beach and made Cadmus and his companions welcome. When they heard the reason which had brought him they made him more welcome still, offered to look after his three ships and as many of his followers as he wished at Cirrha until his return from Apollo's Oracle at Delphi.

'And if Apollo of the Golden Bow bids you go perform any labour alone', they ended, 'do not fear for the safety of your comrades left behind with us, or of the divine Harmonia, your bride-to-be. For we will treat them as our honoured guests, and guard them from any who would work them evil. Even though you are gone for a Divine Year – for eight years and a month, as men reckon time – still you shall find them safe at the end of it, if we can achieve it, and if none of the Immortals will it otherwise. For who can stand against the Immortal gods – whether it be Poseidon, the Shaker of the Earth overwhelming us with a great wave of the sea; whether it be Apollo and his sister Artemis the Huntress shooting us with the arrows of sickness; or whether great Zeus himself cast a thunderbolt upon us – or send his son Hermes, the Guide of the Dead, to lead any man or woman whose hour has come, down to dark Realm of Hades?'

So Cadmus set out from Cirrha with twenty-five of his companions – the half of a ship's crew – leaving the rest to guard his own two ships and that which Electra and Emathion had given to Harmonia. Over the level plain they went for a little while, beneath the shade of great groves of olive trees, walking in a silver twilight as the sun glinted on their leaves. Presently they began to climb as their path led them up the steep valley of the River Pleistos by a winding track on the left of the stream; and after two hours climb they came to a ridge from which, looking back they could see the wide Bay of Cirrha and their own ships lying on the beach, made small as toys by the distance.

Then they turned and followed the path round the edge of the ridge, with the sheer cliffs of Parnassus towering above them, scarcely a hundred yards away – and came to the Temple of Apollo near to where the Fountain of Castalia gushes out of the rock beside a chasm where, in the early days of the world, Apollo had slain the Dragon Python, whose breath still steamed up through a cleft in the rock over which the temple was built. And when Cadmus had made known the reason for his coming, he was led into the temple where the priestess of the Oracle sat on a golden tripod beyond the thin haze of steam that came up from the crack in the rocky floor.

Usually when suppliants came to consult his Oracle at Delphi, Apollo spoke in the voice of his priestess, the Pythia, strange words that the priests took down and interpreted; but this time the Immortal son of Zeus spoke clearly and in his own voice:

'Cadmus, your quest is vain – the quest on which you set forth from distant Sidon. You sought for a bull that was the calf of no earthly cow: you sought for your sister Europa whose happy fortune it is to found a great nation in Crete. Forget about Sidon and the land of your father Agenor. Forget the bull you were following, and instead follow a cow! When you leave my Temple, go down into the valley and turn to the east. On the hillside higher up the River Pleistos you will find a herd of cattle grazing. This belongs to Pelagon of Phocis. Among them you will find a heifer marked on each side with the likeness of a full moon. Purchase this heifer from Pelagon and follow her day and night, taking care not to chase or frighten her in any way. Where she lies down, there found your city – the city that in after days shall be called Thebes. And in memory of the young cow which led you, the land shall be called Boeotia – the Cow Land – ever after. When the heifer has led you to your future home, sacrifice her to me and to Athena – and take whatever may befall thereafter.'

All this Cadmus did as he was commanded by the voice of Apollo. With his companions he made his way down the Castalian stream almost to its junction with the River Pleistos, and then he turned east up the valley and came before long to the great sloping meadows of Anemoria, which is today called Arachova, and there he found the herds of Pelagon grazing. The heifer with the likeness of the full moon on either flank was easily found and bought, and soon they were on their way up the valley, following where it led.

But now began the most wearisome part of their strange quest. The heifer was obviously in no hurry; she stopped often to graze or to drink at a stream: but she never seemed to grow tired – and she certainly never showed any desire to lie down. On she went, indeed, up the steep valley to the Cleft Way of Schiste, where three roads meet, which was to be the place of doom for certain of the descendants of Cadmus; and then north-east of Daulis where also terrible things were to take place in days to come. By Panopaeus, from the red earth of which Prometheus the Good Titan had first formed man, they went; by Chaironea and by Coronia; by Haliartos and by Thespiai – until at last they reached a strange foot-hill of the high range of Mount Kithairon. This foot-hill ran many miles out into the plain, and there ended abruptly in a flat rocky knoll with shallow valleys on either side, rather like a headland sticking out into a lake or into a wide gulf of the sea.

Here the heifer lay down suddenly on the very summit of this inland cape.

For a while Cadmus stood on the highest rock surveying the scene of his future home. Away to the south towered the range of Mount Kithairon joined by a long, low neck of land to the mount on which he stood; and on either side streams flowed down towards the distant Lake Copais in the fertile plain which stretched almost as far as he could see, with the mountains of Ptous and Orchomenus rising to form a background, with the great range of Parnassus away to the west, and a glimpse of the sea to the north east towards Euboea.

It seemed a fair land, and Cadmus felt his heart swell with pride as he surveyed it.

Presently he turned to his companions and cried: 'Behold the home which Zeus has given to us! Here on this mount I will build my citadel – and I shall call it Cadmeia! But first of all, let us sacrifice this heifer to the Immortals as Apollo bade us.'

So, while some killed and cut up the heifer, others gathered wood to make a fire, while others again made their way down to the stream on the west to bring water for the ceremony and for the meal that was to follow it. For it was necessary that Cadmus should cleanse his hands and then pour pure water over the sacrifice: for at that time there was no wine known in the land of Greece, since Dionysus the Lord of the Vine was not yet born.

The men who went for the water had not been gone for long when Cadmus heard them shouting for help and screaming as if in mortal terror. Drawing his sword he rushed down the slope towards the stream, followed by most of those men who had remained with him to prepare the sacrifice. At the head of the narrow valley the water gushed out of the rock which rose sheer behind it for a dozen feet or more. In the rock was a dark cave.

But Cadmus saw neither the fountain nor the cave – for a terrible creature whose home was in the cave was attacking the men who had gone for water, and already two lay dead, horribly torn by its great fangs. Even as Cadmus reached it, the Dragon seized another man in its jaws, pouring out a green foam which seemed to freeze his body for a moment before the deadly poison ate into it like strong acid into metal.

With a cry of rage Cadmus sprang at the Dragon and struck at its scaley neck with his sword. But the blade turned ringing in his hand and a moment later the Dragon's snakey tail was creeping round his legs, round his body, binding him in fetters from which it seemed there was no escape.

But as he strained against the horrible death closing tighter and tighter round him, it seemed to Cadmus that suddenly Pallas Athena stood before him, the warrior daughter of Zeus, the Immortal Lady of Wisdom:

'Courage, Cadmus!' she seemed to cry. 'Do not you, who helped Zeus to overcome Typhon, allow a mere Dragon to overcome you! Not Ares the War-God himself can save it from you, though his it is! Strive as you never strove before – and when the Dragon lies dead, take its teeth and sow them in the plain beneath – and the crop of Spartoi, the Sown Men, shall replace those whom the Dragon has slain and give you Earth-born ancestors for many of the mighty heroes of Thebes who are to be!'

At these words such strength came upon Cadmus that with a shout he tore the Dragon's coils from him and sprang back out of its reach.

Hissing terribly, it came at him once more, smashing a man's skull with one blow of its tail as it passed. But Cadmus stooped and tore up from the ground a great mass of jagged rock and flung it with such strength at the Dragon's head that it fell back stunned and bleeding – just long enough for Cadmus to snatch up his sword and strike it so fiercely across the soft, unprotected throat, that he well-nigh severed the head. And the Dragon writhed and curled for a little while only, before it lay dead.

As the Dragon died the poisonous fumes from its breath seemed to cloud his mind once more: but Cadmus no longer saw the beautiful Athena, strong and calm and austere in her shinning armour of wisdom untroubled by the passions against which mortals find it so hard to arm themselves. Instead, the very Lord of War, the Immortal Ares towered over him – a warrior against whom no man might dream of standing.

'Cadmus, Dragon killer!' cried Ares – and his voice was as that of one who cries aloud in anger to be heard above the tumult of the fiercest battle – 'Cadmus, murderer of my serpent! You cannot escape the punishment that is your due for slaying this my servant. But I know all that you have done in Thrace and, with the rest of the Immortal gods who dwell on Olympus, I praise and honour you. Yet justice must be done: but it shall be the mildest that may be. For slaying my Dragon you must serve me for one Divine Year: for eight years and one month as you mortals reckon time. But it shall not be until your days on earth are ended. Far in the north that day shall come – and it shall come to my daughter, Harmonia, your bride to be, at the same moment. Then for that one Divine Year you shall both serve me in the guise of serpents: and when that year is ended, in your own forms grown young and glorious you shall enter together into the paradise of the Heroes, the Elysian Fields in the Islands of the Blessed beyond the world's end.'

Then all seemed to spin; and the next thing he remembered was the cold, clear water of the Fountain being splashed in his face by his men to revive him.

Very soon Cadmus had recovered from the battle and returned to complete the sacrifice which the Dragon had interrupted. But when that was ended he remembered the strange command which Pallas Athena had given him during his struggle against death, and he made haste back to where the shimmering corpse of the Dragon lay. The head had almost been cut off by his last great blow, and it was an easy matter to cut through the creature's spine and bear away the trophy in triumph. As it proved difficult to extract the teeth one by one, Cadmus had his men place the whole head in a cauldron of water over a smouldering fire and leave it there all night.

Next day the great skull was boiled clean of all the flesh and scales, and it was easy to pull out the rows of sharp teeth from the bare jaw-bones. When he had them all, Cadmus led the way down to the nearest stretch of level land. There were peasants living in huts nearby who willingly brought out a wooden plough, harnessed two oxen to it, and ploughed up a stretch of the field. Then Cadmus took the Dragon's teeth in a bronze helmet and strode up and down the field scattering them right and left as a farmer scatters the seed-corn.

But these seeds needed no spring showers nor summer suns to make them flourish and ripen. Scarcely had Cadmus come to the end of the furrow and turned to look back and see what might happen, when armed men began to grow out of the earth – one where each of the Dragon's teeth had fallen. First from the furrows there came the points of spears; and then helmets with waving plumes; then bronze clad shoulders and soon a band of warriors stood there in a line, knocking their feet free from the clinging soil and dusting it from their curved shields and shining greaves.

Cadmus stood amazed, not knowing what to do, and the Sown Men seemed bemused also. But suddenly, as if they had only just seen him, they gathered into a compact body and charged towards him, shouting and waving their swords. Scarcely realising what he did, Cadmus picked up a jagged rock and hurled it into their midst.

At once they turned upon each other crying: 'You dare to strike me? Take that' – 'You think you can do what you like to me – I'll show you how wrong you are', and suchlike words – and began to fight furiously among themselves.

Very soon all but five lay dead. Then these suddenly stopped fighting, sheathed their swords, and came towards Cadmus with open hands in token of peace.

'I am Echion the Snake-man', said the first of the Sown Men, 'and my companions are called Udaeus, the Ground-man; Chthonius, the Earth-born; Hyperenor, the Over-bearing and Pelorus, the Monster-man. The strength of the Earth is in our limbs and the fierceness of Ares in our hearts. We have been sent to help you in your task of founding a great city here – and here, Cadmus, we choose you to be our king and swear loyalty to you.'

So, without more ado, Cadmus marked out the bounds of the Cadmeia, the citadel of what would be the city of Thebes – on the headland with the Dragon's stream on one side and the Ismenean Stream on the other, and began to build a mighty wall round it. And in this the five Sown Men proved by far the best labourers, for, although not much above the common height, they seemed to have the strength of giants – and with their aid Cadmus built round the Cadmeia a wall of mighty many-shaped boulders and half-hewn stones such as the Titans had built about Mycenae and Tiryns where they stand to this day.

When the Cadmeia was built, with streets and houses, and a palace in the midst, Cadmus sent to Cirrha for Harmonia and the rest of his men. These came joyfully, bringing with them the three wooden figure-heads from the ships to set up in the Shrine of Aphrodite in their new city – two statues from Sidon and one from Samothrace. During their long wait at Cirrha many of the men who had followed Cadmus all the way from Phoenecia had found wives for themselves among the maidens of Cirrha, of nearby Amphissa, and of Delphi. Some were engaged to the maidens who tended on Harmonia and who would not wed before their mistress; and already new citizens had come to dwell in or near the Cadmeia, with their wives and families – shepherds who dwelt on the slopes of Kithairon, fisher-folk who made their living on the shores of Lake Copais, and others from the plain who served no over-lord or wished to leave those whom they did serve in Thespiai or Orchomenos.

As soon as all was ready, the day came for the wedding of Cadmus and Harmonia – and, as he had promised, Zeus came with the other Immortals to sit upon golden thrones in the Cadmeia and bring more renown to that feast than any other mortal was to know – save only the hero Peleus when he married the sea-nymph Thetis, they who became the parents of the great Achilles.

First came the Nine Muses from Mount Helicon, playing the marriage hymn, while the Three Graces celebrated the event with dances. Then came lovely Aphrodite herself to decorate the bridal bower for Harmonia; and with her came Ares all unarmed to dance at his daughter's wedding as a father should.

Dancing too came Apollo, while he passed the golden plectrum over the seven strings of his lyre, bringing forth music more ravishingly lovely than any mortal heard before. And as he played, Polymnia, the Muse of the Divine Song sang the bridal hymn, while Terpsichore, Muse of the Choral Dance led them in time to the music and the song.

Then as Zeus and Hera, Poseidon and Demeter and the rest of the Imortals seated themselves on the golden thrones about the royal hearth of Cadmus where the feast was held, a light shone in that hall which made dim the torches: it was as if dawn had come to that house alone, long before night was done.

The true dawn was beginning to flush the eastern sky over distant Parnes mountains before that feast ended and the Immortals returned to Olympus. But before they went each in turn gave gifts to bride and bridegroom: Zeus granted them long years of success in all they strove to do; Demeter laid her blessing on the soil of Boeotia, so that the corn might grow more richly there than in any other part of Greece; Poseidon, Lord of the Sea, granted fertility to the creatures both of the sea and of the fresh-water – fat mullets in the Euboean Gulf and the great, tasty eels that were to make Lake Copais famous.

Hera herself gave them a throne studded with jewels; Hermes gave a lyre which he had invented for Apollo, and Apollo himself a bow; Athena gave to Harmonia a golden cloak and Hephaestus set a jewel-studded coronet on her head. But Aphrodite herself waited until all the rest had given their gifts and then stepping forward with a bewitching smile she clasped round Harmonia's throat a necklace of gold and jewels more lovely than any this Earth had seen, saying as she did so:

'My child, take this Necklace as my gift – and with it the gift of beauty. Earthly beauty must fade – but this Necklace shall wake irresistible desire – as indeed the gift of Aphrodite should.'

Then, laughing softly, she led them to the bridal bower and closed the door behind them, and passed away to her own place, still laughing.

But this Necklace of Harmonia was destined to breed desires that would bring many a sorrow to all who wore it in the days to come – and great woes upon the city of Thebes itself.

Jael Jordan

IV

THE BIRTH OF DIONYSUS

After their marriage Cadmus and Harmonia reigned for many long and prosperous years over their new kingdom, and found complete happiness together in their palace on the Cadmeia, the site of which is marked today by the market place of Thebes.

But that happiness was not to last even to the end of their lives – long though that was. It seemed, in spite of all that Zeus owed to Cadmus for his help in the war with Typhon, that even he could not keep back the decree of the Fates: for Fate is more powerful even than the Lord of Olympus himself.

Harmonia had already given the fatal Necklace, the gift of jealous Aphrodite, to her youngest daughter Semele and so brought upon her, unwanted, the love of Zeus himself; but he, Zeus, saw all that was to come to pass and, as so often, was forced to sacrifice the happiness of a few for the good of very many. And so it came about that Zeus fell in love with Semele, the fourth daughter of Cadmus and Harmonia, and came to visit her secretly in the very room in the palace which had once been her parents' bridal chamber.

Cadmus and Harmonia had been blessed with five children: Agave, Ino, Autonoe and Semele, and a son born after all the rest who was called Polydorus. Agave had married Echion, the leader of the Sown Men and, according to the Greek custom, they took over the rule from Cadmus as soon as he began to grow old – though he was still King in name, and still held the ultimate power. When Polydorus was born, they ruled the land as before, but were bound by oath to hand it over to him as soon as he came of age.

But that was many years in the future when Zeus began to visit

Semele: for Polydorus was then still only a baby, just beginning to toddle about the palace and speak his first words.

Zeus first saw Semele when she was bathing in the River Asopus that flows from Kithairon to the north of Thebes along below Parnes into the distant sea near Oropus, making there the boundary between Boeotia and Attica – the kingdoms of Thebes and Athens. Taking the form of an eagle he skimmed down low over the water, and saw that she was indeed as lovely and irresistible as Aphrodite when she first rose from the sea beside the shores of Cyprus.

Then Zeus knew that here was the fated mother of Dionysus, youngest of the Great Gods, the Lord of Delight, giver of the joys of wine; and that night he came to the Palace of Cadmus wrapped in a Cloak of Darkness so that none might see him pass. As he came to the outer gates of the Cadmeia they opened before him and closed after him so swiftly and silently that the very guards saw and heard nothing.

Into the palace he came, and, once again none saw him nor did any door remain shut when he would pass through it. At length he came to the room where lovely Semele lay alone sleeping at first a dreamless sleep. But in a little while it seemed to her that a man stood beside her bed whose head was that of a horned bull. And then he turned into a shaggy lion; and into a lithe panther. Then he was a young man of exceeding beauty with vine-leaves twined in his hair from which a snake came gliding down onto her bed with a gentle hiss that became a kind of bridal hymn. All this caused her no fear at all, but only an exultation and a thrilling knowledge that she stood upon the very edge of Mystery. Without forming the thoughts in her mind she knew that she was seeing both the Immortal who loved her and the Immortal who was to be her son – Dionysus of the many forms, the bull, the lion, the ivy-wreathed youth, the giver of joys to mankind: Dionysus of the many names – Bacchus, Bromios, Bassarios and the mystic Zagreus.

The snake glided into her arms telling her of all this without words and then murmuring 'It is I, Zeus, who holds you', even as it turned from snake into man and their lips met.

Then it seemed that all earth laughed for joy; that vines grew suddenly around and over Semele's bed; that the walls were draped with flowers and the roof beams hung with clusters of grapes . . .

When the first pale light of dawn began to creep into the room,

Jael Jordan

Semele woke to find the shadowy figure of a man in the very prime of manhood standing beside her.

'Do not be afraid', he said, in a voice that filled her at once with a great fear and greater peace. 'I, your husband, am none other than Zeus himself. Be proud that you have been chosen for this great honour – and be assured that no child born of mortal woman shall be as great as yours. Your father's sister Europa was chosen for a like destiny: Minos and Rhadamanthys, her sons, shall live for ever – yes – but in the Realm of Hades, as Judges of the Dead. But your son Dionysus shall come to dwell for ever with his fellow gods in Olympus. Do not reproach me if terrible things befall you in this world and if you dwell for a space among the Dead: the time shall come when Dionysus your son will bring you to the eternal dwellings of the Immortals. Do not grieve that much sorrow must come upon you and each of your sisters. Rejoice and be happy, most fortunate of mortal women. You will be the mother of a son who will help mortals to forget their troubles and bring joy both to gods and men.'

Then he faded from her sight, and Semele slept, and woke – and for a little while did not know whether it had all been a dream. And a dream it seemed night after night when Zeus visited her in his assumed form, and she saw him only for a moment in the flickering lamp-light at his coming, and again in the first pale light of dawn when he left her in the morning.

But as the months passed and she knew that she was destined to bear a child to this strange midnight lover, Semele was not untroubled by doubts whether it was in truth Zeus who visited her nightly. And she could not but realise that her faithful handmaidens Peisianassa and Thelxinoe did not believe her tale of an Immortal but were discussing together which of the young men of Cadmeia was deceiving their mistress.

When jealous Hera perceived these doubts beginning to cloud Semele's brow, she saw her course clearly. As with Io, Hera found herself unable to react in any other way than a mortal woman would – and, forgetting all that was fated to come of this divine unfaithfulness, she set about the destruction of her rival. Yet she knew that she must hide her part in Semele's fate from Zeus, who could punish her most terribly if so he willed, Immortal though she was.

Hera could not change her shape as Zeus could, but she soon thought of another method of disguise. Mounting her peacock-drawn chariot she sped through the upper air until she came to the island of Crete. Here, on the hillside above Amnisos, she came to the cave where her daughter Eileithyia, Goddess of Childbirth, had herself been born. Eileithyia dwelt there no longer, for indeed there was no rest for her anywhere in the world; but in the cave dwelt Apate, the spirit of Deceit, who was her faithful servant.

'Greetings, Lady of wily mind, nymph of all wily snares', she said. 'I come to beg of you the loan of your girdle of many colours so that with it I may deceive a worthless mortal woman who has taken my husband whom even the goddess Leto, mother of Apollo and Artemis, could not steal for more than a single night.'

'Mother of Eileithyia, bride of Zeus', answered Apate, 'surely I will give you my girdle and anything else you may ask of me. I obey, since with Zeus you reign over gods and men. Take this sash bind it about you, and you may deceive any mortal – you may perhaps deceive even Zeus himself – for it is more powerful even than the heart-bewitching girdle of Aphrodite.'

So Hera took the many-coloured sash of Deceit and sped swiftly to the palace on the Cadmeia. There, full of guile, she made all believe that she was Beroe, an ancient crone whom Cadmus had brought with him and who once had been his nurse many years ago in distant Sidon.

Semele herself was completely deceived and received the wizened old dame kindly. She helped her to her straight-backed chair of ebony inlaid with ivory and, setting a soft cushion of sheepskin stuffed with wool on its seat for her, sent Peisianassa for a rug and Thelxinoe for fruit and milk.

Presently the disguised Hera found her opportunity and said: 'Tell me, my queen, why are your cheeks so pale? Why is your beauty fading? Is it because of the wicked rumours which are being whispered all over the city? They say that you have a lover – a wild man from the mountains who dares to pretend that he is one of the Immortals who dwell on Olympus.'

Semele murmured something about being certain that it was indeed one of the deathless gods, and Hera cut in quickly:

'Well, it is easy to prove – since I see that even you yourself are not quite certain. If it is Ares who has wedded you in secret, tell him to come to you in his flashing armour as he came to Aphrodite – and not like a thief skulking through the night. If it be

Poseidon of the sea-blue hair, let him come with trident in hand as he came to Amphitrite in the deep caves of the ocean. If Zeus himself is your lover, let him come in his majesty as when he visits gold-shod Hera; and if it is shining Apollo, make him come to you through the air drawn in his car by singing swans.'

Speaking in this way the false Beroe made poor Semele more and more uncertain and doubtful, less inclined to trust in the word of her divine lover, and increasingly anxious to prove to the world – and to herself – that he was indeed Zeus.

Accordingly, next time the shadowy figure came to visit her, Semele begged him to grant her a boon – one wish for whatever she might choose.

Suspecting no ill, Zeus replied: 'Whatever you will shall be yours, and I swear to refuse you nothing. Yes, I swear by Styx, the River of Death; that oath which the very gods cannot break.'

'Then, if you are Zeus indeed, come to me in your majesty as you come to Hera, Queen of Heaven!' cried Semele.

When he heard this, Zeus saw the cruel web which the Fates had woven, and how Hera had sought vengeance by destroying Semele through this mad wish. But he could not break his oath, and so he turned sadly from Semele, saying: 'My beloved mortal bride, the jealous mind of Hera has deceived you by a trick. Do you really think that my thunders can be gentle? Do you think that I visited Io or Europa – or even Leto, who was herself an Immortal – as I visit Hera?'

But foolish Semele was not to be dissuaded. So Zeus went back to Olympus, wrapped himself in his awful majesty of thunder and lightning, and tore through the sky and back into the palace of Cadmus like a thunderbolt.

As the roof of her chamber burst open in a blinding flash of fire Semele held up her arms towards her death crying:

'I am indeed the bride of Zeus! Listen to the thunder: it is my marriage hymn! Behold the lightning: it kindles my bridal torches! Ah, Zeus! – '

But even as he stood before her the fire turned her to ashes and the wing of the palace roared up in flames.

But Zeus was mindful of his son who was to be Dionysus the giver of joy to mankind. Even as Semele's ashes fell to the ground, Zeus caught up the half-formed baby whom the fire could not harm, and hid him – gashing his own thigh and sewing him away out of sight until he should grow strong and big enough to survive in the hard world of mortal men.

When this time was come, Zeus undid the stitches and carried the baby Dionysus to Autonoe and Ino, the sisters of Semele, bidding them bring up the child with their own children – but disguised as a girl.

Now Autonoe, the eldest, took the Necklace of Harmonia which had been given to Semele, and said to her sister Ino:

'You must guard the child and bring him up with your own Learchus and Melicertes, for they are still young. My son Actaeon is already nearing manhood, and it would look strange for me suddenly to be nursing a new baby: too many questions would be asked – and Aristaeus my husband would find them hard to answer.'

So Ino took the baby Dionysus away with her to Coroneia, twenty miles to the west of Thebes, where she and her husband Athamas of Orchonomenos dwelt in his little kingdom beneath the slopes of Mount Laphistios. There he remained safely for a while, tended by Ino who let it be thought that a baby daughter had been born to her and Athamas while she was on a long visit to her sisters at Thebes.

But Autonoe spread another rumour in Thebes – that Semele had been killed by a thunderbolt hurled by Zeus who was angered because she had pretended that her mortal lover was Zeus himself; and that she and her lover had been burnt to ashes in the fire which consumed one wing of the palace on the Cadmeia.

Autonoe, the eldest child of Cadmus and Harmonia, had long been married to Aristaeus the Wandering Healer. He was the son of the nymph Cyrene and Apollo. The God of the Bow had rescued Cyrene from a lion which she was fighting courageously on Mount Pelion, far to the north of Thebes, and carried her away to found the city called after her in North Africa. But Aristaeus, when he grew up, came wandering back to his mother's homeland and, guided by Apollo learnt the art of healing from the wise Cheiron, the half-man-half-horse Centaur who dwelt in a cave on Pelion and was the wisest creature upon earth.

And when he had learnt all that Cheiron could teach him of the healer's art, and much too of the skills of the husbandman and the weather-prophet, Apollo led Aristaeus to the Cadmeia, and Cadmus and Harmonia were well pleased to have such a husband for their eldest daughter.

They had one son called Actaeon, who spent most of his time with a pack of savage deer-hounds, hunting on Mount Kithairon a little to the south of the Cadmeia, where he became famous as a hunter even while he was still a boy.

Actaeon grew into a remarkably handsome young man, and his mother Autonoe, made vain perhaps by the baleful magic of the Necklace of Harmonia, soon turned his head completely.

'My sister Semele was loved by Zeus himself', she said, 'though that is a secret you must tell to nobody. And her mother and mine is the daughter of Ares and Aphrodite. So you see you are almost one of the Immortals yourself – and only an Immortal is worthy to be your wife.'

'True indeed', agreed Actaeon arrogantly. 'And of the Immortals the only one for me is Artemis, the virgin huntress. She too follows the deer on Kithairon: I have seen her there many times, and indeed we have hunted together. Her swift arrows and my sharp spear have laid low both bears and lions on the mountain heights – both she and I together have outrun the fastest stag and brought it to bay. Yes, Artemis and no other shall be my bride!'

So saying, Actaeon went forth to win his chosen bride, and for many days he and his pack of hounds hunted over Mount Kithairon in vain. But he began to boast that he was hunting not the wild beasts of the mountains but Artemis the goddess of all wild beasts instead – and very soon the Dryad nymphs who dwell in the trees and the Naiad nymphs who had the streams and rivers in their care, told the goddess of Actaeon's boast.

Artemis, the virgin huntress, who would never wed either mortal or Immortal, was justly angered. But before she could punish him in any way Actaeon brought his own doom upon himself by breaking the law of heaven and earth that any mortal who looked upon an Immortal without the Immortal's will – even if he did so only by chance – must die or at the very least be struck blind.

There was a pool of clear water high upon Kithairon, hidden by sheer rocks and screened by mighty oak trees. This Actaeon knew to be a favourite resort of the goddess, and here he determined to lie in wait for her. So during the heat of the summer afternoon when all sensible mortals lay down to sleep for an hour or two until the cool of evening, Actaeon climbed into a big oak tree from which he had a good view of the pool, laid himself down along a branch, and waited.

Before very long there came the sound of the chase, and then Artemis came speeding into the glade by the pool. At a wave of her hand the hounds were led away by her attendant nymphs, and she turned suddenly, cast her garments – the short skirt and bodice of soft doe-skin – from her, and stepped into the pool.

Actaeon gazed greedily down, drinking in the naked loveliness that no man might see and live. Then a Naiad nymph saw him and shrieked out. Artemis slipped into the water just as Actaeon sprang down from his tree, came towards her and knelt humbly beside the pool, beginning to explain that he had come only to visit her and tell her of a noble lion on Mount Parnes that they might hunt together – and had never intended to offend her as he had done.

But Artemis, flushing red with anger and with shame, cast a handful of water into his face which blinded him for a moment, crying:

'Now you are free to go and tell all your people that you have seen Artemis naked – if you are allowed to tell anything, you who dared also to boast that you would take me, the Unwed, to be your wife!'

A blind terror seized upon Actaeon. Without a word he turned and fled away, crashing through the thickets on the mountainside. Presently he heard his own hounds baying in the distance, and called to them. They were the last words that he ever spoke, for even as they passed his lips the words became blurred and he suddenly found that he was not shouting like a man but belling like a stag.

He looked down at his feet and saw to his horror that they were changing into cloven hooves. Stooping, he felt his legs – and they were the hairy legs of a stag. And now, having stooped he could not rise again but fell forward on his hands, only to find that they too were turning into hooves. In front of him was a tiny pool of water, scarcely more than a puddle, but a perfect mirror. He leant over this – and saw the antlered head of a stag looking up at him.

Then Actaeon wept aloud – the great tears chasing one another down his hairy cheeks – and tried to call upon Artemis, upon any of the Immortals for help, for forgiveness.

But there was no forgiveness. Very soon he heard his own hounds drawing near. They at least, he felt, would still be his friends. But the hounds saw only a stag standing before them, heard only a stag belling desperately and, as they had been taught to do, they tore him to pieces.

After they had done this the hounds ran on, seeking in vain for their master; and at last they came to Cheiron's cave on Mount Pelion, and the kindly Centaur, having discovered what had happened, was able by his arts to bring them forgetfulness of their lost master and of any half-knowledge of what they had done.

As for Aristaeus and Autonoe, they too sought far and wide for their lost son, until Zeus took pity on them and sent his Messenger to tell them what had befallen him and show them the bones of the stag which had once been Actaeon.

Feeling that she was partly to blame for his terrible end, Autonoe fled away from Boeotia and passed the rest of her days in the land of the Megarians near Athens. And when she died they buried her in the village of Eveneia where she had lived, and raised a tomb over her which was venerated for centuries to come.

As for Aristaeus, he set out for Delphi to ask his father Apollo what he should do now that he had lost both wife and son. And Apollo bade him go first to the island of Ceos and teach the people there those arts of husbandry which he had discovered and taught the Boetians – how to make cheese, how to keep bees, and how to shelter the crops from the burning heat of the sun – and then to return to Cyrene in Libya where he was born, and teach these arts to the people of his mother's own city. And for his gifts to mankind he was honoured ever after as a demi-god, most especially in Boeotia, Ceos and Cyrene, and in the other places where he had taught, such as Thrace and Sicily and Sardinia.

When she went into exile in Eveneia, Autonoe left the Necklace of Harmonia behind in the Cadmeia, and the curse which accompanied it remained behind also and fell next upon Ino – though she was still living with her husband King Athamas at Coroneia.

Certain it is that Ino suddenly began to grow jealous of her step-children Phrixus and Helle. For Athamas had first married Nephele, the Cloud-nymph, whom he had met on Mount Laphystios; and they had lived happily together at Coroneia for some years.

But then Athamas fell in love with Ino the daughter of Cadmus, and Nephele, seeing that she could not compete with an earthly princess, fled away up Mount Laphystios and into the sky to join her sister Clouds. So Athamas married Ino, and they had two sons called Learchus and Melicertes, with whom the infant Dionysus was being brought up as a little girl.

Ino's jealousy of Phrixus and Helle grew by leaps and bounds. Soon she began to weave plots against them, and finally hit upon a scheme in which she persuaded most of the women of Coroneia to help her. They parched the seed-corn during the winter so that when it was sown no wheat grew and the earth remained barren.

Thinking that some curse had come upon his land, Athamas sent messengers to Delphi to ask the Oracle of Apollo how it might be lifted. But Ino chose the messengers, and they returned with a lying take that the curse could only be lifted if Athamas sacrificed his son Phrixus to Zeus on the top of Mount Laphystios.

When Athamas heard this, he wept and lamented – and refused to obey the Oracle. But Ino made sure that it was made known to all the people of Coroneia, and they came in a crowd to the palace declaring that they would sacrifice Athamas himself, and then Phrixus after him, if he did not obey the command of Apollo.

So Athamas was forced to lead the sorrowing procession to the summit of Laphystios where an altar was built on which Phrixus was laid.

But at the last moment, when the knife was raised to kill him, Nephele swooped down out of the sky with a Golden Ram on which she set both Phrixus and Helle. Then the magic Ram with the fleece of gold flew away over land and sea with the two children on its back. As they passed over the southern end of the straits between Europe and Asia, Helle fell off and was drowned – and it has been called the Hellespont, Helle's Sea, after her ever since. But Phrixus flew safely on until he came to Colchis at the furthest end of the known world. There King Aeetes the Wizard welcomed him, sacrificed the Ram and hung the Golden Fleece on a tree in a secret grove: and there it remained until Jason and the Argonauts came in quest of it.

The people of Coroneia did not sacrifice Athamas in place of Phrixus, but they passed a strange law that if he or his eldest male descendant set foot in the Bouleterion, the Town Hall, of Coroneia, he should be sacrificed at once on Mount Laphystios: and this custom was observed for more than a thousand years.

But Athamas himself was not likely to enter the Bouleterion of Coroneia himself. For when he discovered what Ino had done, madness came upon him. Seizing his bow and arrows he set out to slay Ino and her two children, crying:

'Come with me, my comrades of the hunt! There is a lioness with her two cubs in my very palace! Come and help me catch and kill them! Bring nets and spears! Bring sharp arrows and your strongest bows!'

Ino sought desperately to escape, crying to the palace servants to hold the mad man back and bind him with ropes until the frenzy left him. But before anyone could reach him Athamas had fitted an arrow to his bow and sent it through the heart of Learchus, the elder of the two sons whom Ino had born him.

'A kill!' he cried. 'See, I have shot one of the cubs! Now for the lioness herself!'

But Ino had had time to catch up, the baby Melicertes in her arms, and dash out of the palace, away through the streets of Coroneia and up into the forests on the Kithairon mountains. But Athamas was following her, and it seemed that escape was impossible. By day and night he pursued her wherever she sought to hide – over Kithairon and down to Aegosthena at the head of the Gulf of Corinth; over the mountains of Megara, by Pagae and Eveneia, until she came to the Molurian rocks on the edge of the Saronic Gulf that lies between Attica and Argolis.

Athamas was now close behind her. With a yell of triumph he set an arrow on his bow string and began to draw. But before he could loose it Ino, with one last despairing cry, cast herself over the cliff edge and into the sea with Melicertes still in her arms.

Some say that Poseidon took pity on Ino and Melicertes and turned them into demi-gods of the sea, giving them the names of Leucothea and Palaemon. But others say that only Melicertes was saved, being carried by a dolphin to the nearby Isthmus of Corinth, where the Isthmian Games were founded by him or in his honour.

Athamas, however, ceased to be mad as soon as his wife and son had disappeared into the sea. Knowing that he would be banished from Boeotia for the murder of his other son, he made his way to Delphi to ask Apollo what he should do, and the Oracle replied:

'Wander on to the north until beasts invite you to dinner!'

Thinking sadly that he was doomed to wander for the rest of his life, Athamas made his way by Schiste and Daulis northwards toward the great plains of Thessaly. Here one day he found some wolves who had just killed a sheep and were beginning to feast on it; seeing him, they drew aside without attempting to attack him and waited until he had cut off a good joint for himself before going on with their meal.

This, Athamas felt sure, was the place meant by the Oracle, so he settled there, and in course of time built the town of Athamantia, married a princess called Themisto, and had four sons to secure him a happy old age.

When Ino left Boeotia the Necklace passed to Agave, the only remaining daughter of Cadmus and Harmonia, whose husband Echion, one of the Sown Men, now ruled in place of Cadmus. To her the child Dionysus was now entrusted; but very soon she proved herself to be an untrustworthy guardian. For she had never really believed that Zeus and not some mortal adventurer, had been Semele's lover; and now she began to let idle words fall about the little boy, 'her dead sister's child', whom she was bringing up as a girl.

Eris, the Goddess of Strife, Hera's favourite daughter, soon told all this to her mother who, jealous as ever, began to suspect that Agave's adopted 'daughter' was none other than Dionysus himself. So she began to plot how she might destroy him completely, and be rid of him once and for all.

But Zeus discovered her plans just in time, and with his help Hermes turned little Dionysus into a young goat, carried him away to mount Nysa in Asia Minor, and hid him in a secluded glen, where the nymphs of Nysa, the Hyades, took care of him until he had grown into a handsome young man.

And for this Zeus turned them into stars and set them to shine for ever in the night sky.

V

THE RETURN OF DIONYSUS

On Mount Nysa the young Dionysus grew safely and speedily. While he was still small the Hyades took care of him. But in his boyhood the goddess Rhea, mother of Zeus himself, took charge of his education. Under her instruction he was soon able to drive a chariot drawn by lions or leopards. At the age of nine he began hunting game for himself, running as fast as the hares and pulling down the young stags when their first horns were just showing.

Dionysus knew no fear. He would wander into a lion's den and carry away the cubs, and rob the she-bears of their young: but indeed all wild things grew tame at his touch, and he was able to lead the very lions from the mountain tops to be harnessed to Rhea's chariot, and the panthers and lynxes for his own.

Thus he grew under the care of the stately Goddess of Wild Nature and tended when need be by the Hyades. And when he grew to young manhood he would sport with the Satyrs, the half-wild men of the rocks and their father, cowardly old Silenus – long-living, though not immortal, powers of Nature, who had flat noses and tiny horns on their foreheads among their shaggy locks.

And he had other companions. Some of the Satyrs were wedded to the Oreads, the mountain nymphs, and among their children were several boys of his own age who became playfellows for Dionysus. Chief among these was Ampelus, and with him Dionysus spent many happy days roaming over the mountains of Nysa and Tmolos and bathing during the hot summer days in the River Pactolos that flows by where the city of Sardis was one day to stand – the Pactolos whose sands became rich in gold as a sign that a young god had bathed so often in its stream.

In the winter Dionysus dwelt in the caves with his friends: the Satyrs would hold merry feasts, Ampelos would play sweetly on his pipe, and the nymphs would dance and sing for them. As yet wine was unknown, though the Satyrs seemed almost able to get drunk without it, so wild and fantastic were their gambols, and so frenzied did they become as they capered about the great log fires until they sank down unable to move through sheer exhaustion.

But these happy times came to an end when Dionysus was fully grown. For there was much that Dionysus had to do on earth before he could be received into the company of the other Immortals of Olympus. The first thing to bring about was the making of wine, and Zeus sent Ate, the Goddess of Discord, in the form of a gadfly to sting the wild bull on which Ampelos was riding one day. The bull dashed up a mountain side, flung Ampelos from his back, gored him to death and went on his way.

A Satyr saw what happened and carried the body to Dionysus who, after weeping and lamenting for his lost friend, begged Rhea for ambrosia, the honey-like food of the Immortals, to annoint him, for burial. Mother Rhea poured the sweet-smelling ambrosia over the body as it lay in its grave, and Dionysus heaped in the earth over what had been Ampelos.

At once there grew up from the grave the first grape-vine. In a few minutes it was putting out leaves, and before long great clusters of grapes that ripened as soon as they were fully formed. At once, as if knowing what to do, Dionysus began gathering the grapes, and, with the Satyrs' aid, pressing and turning them into wine. And thereafter he had but to bless a vineyard and the vines which hitherto had born no more grapes than if they had been wild jasmine or convolvolous would turn into grape-vines and begin to grow their clusters of rich black and gold.

Then, instructed by Rhea and at the command of Zeus, Dionysus set out through the world in his chariot attended by the Satyrs to bring the grapes to all men and teach all who would honour him and do him worship how to make wine.

He went even as far as India, and to the sun-baked steppes of Persia, to the deserts of Arabia and to the Ethiopians, and through all the lands of Asia Minor, through Lydia and Phrygia, through Caria and Lycia and Cilicia – until all were won over to his worship and growing the grape-bearing vines and making the heaven-sent wine from their rich crops to be a solace for mankind and a blessed escape from care.

Sometimes the lands to which he came would welcome Dionysus; but some countries tried to fight against him and had to be conquered by force or guile – and by his magic power of turning whatever he touched into a fruitful vine, and of transforming into wine the waters of any spring or river that would serve his purpose.

One king who strove to destroy him was Lycurgus of Thrace – and Dionysus escaped by hiding for a while in the ocean-caves of the sea-nymph Thetis who many years later was destined to become the mother of Achilles. Lycurgus drove out of his country all the followers of Dionysus, the Satyrs and the wild women called Bacchae who joined his train, and imprisoned those Thracians who had accepted him and his teachings.

But while he was dwelling with Thetis, Zeus bestowed upon Dionysus the full powers of an Immortal god of Olympus so that he was able to return unharmed to Thrace and punish Lycurgus who tried again to capture him. For Dionysus drove Lycurgus mad so that he seized an axe and rushed out to cut down the vines. But he mistook his own son Dryas for a vine and cut him in pieces; and finally cut off one of his own feet thinking his leg the stem of another vine. And after this the Thracians, fearing a curse would fall on them, sacrificed Lycurgus on top of Mount Pangaeus, set free his prisoners, and accorded Dionysus full honours as a god.

Dionysus did not remain long with the Thracians. As he walked one day in the likeness of a handsome young man on the sea-shore near Amphipolis where Strymon, the river of Thrace, flows into the sea, a ship came sailing towards him.

Its crew was a gang of Etruscan pirates seeking young men and maidens to capture and sell as slaves. They saw Dionysus, a youth in his first flush of manhood: with his rich dark hair falling over his broad shoulders and his splendid purple robe, he seemed their ideal prey. So they landed and seized him, put him on their ship and sailed away well pleased. But when they tried to bind him the bonds would not hold him, and the cords fell away from his hands and feet, while he sat with a smile in his dark eyes.

Then the helmsman suspected that this must be an Immortal wearing human form, and cried to his fellows: 'Madmen! This is some god you have taken and seek to bind – and he is too strong for you. Surely this is Zeus himself, or Apollo of the silver bow, or sea-blue-haired Poseidon. He does not look like a mortal man but like the gods who dwell on Olympus. Come then, let us set him down on the shore at once: do not lay hands on him or he will grow angry and stir up dangerous winds and heavy squalls.'

So he said. But the Captain jeered at him, crying: 'Idiot! Mind your own business, which is to help hoist the sails, for you see that the wind blows conveniently from the north and will take us on our way. As for this fellow, the rest of us will look after him. Maybe he comes from Egypt or Cyprus – perhaps he may even be a Hyperborean from the Land beyond the North Wind, or further still. But in the end we will make him talk, and find if he comes from a rich family. Then we can rob them and sell them into slavery.'

Having said this, he caused the sails to be hoisted, and the wind filled them, drawing the ship forward at a spanking pace as the crew hauled taut the sheets on either side and cleated them.

But soon strange things began to happen. First of all fragrant sweet wine began to flow in the scuppers instead of water and a heavenly scent arose to the amazement of all who smelt and saw it. Then suddenly a vine grew up the mast and spread out along the tops of the sails with thick clusters of grapes hanging from it everywhere, while flowers and tendrils twined round all the tholepins.

When the pirates saw all this, they at last agreed that the helmsman was right, and one and all begged him to turn the ship and steer for land. But on the instant Dionysus transformed himself into a fierce lion and stood in the bows of the ship roaring loudly, and the pirates fled confusedly to the stern and all tried to hide behind the helmsman as the only right-minded man amongst them. The lion, however, charged down the ship as if to sieze the Captain, and all but the helmsman leapt screaming into the sea and were turned into dolphins.

Then Dionysus changed back into the form of the handsome young man crowned with vine-leaves and clapped the helmsman on the back, saying:

'Take good heart, my friend, for you have found favour with me and shall be the first of my priests. For know that I am Dionysus, Bacchus of the loud cry, Bromios the wine-giver! I am the son of mighty Zeus, and my mother was Semele the daughter of Cadmus.

I go now to seek the land where I was born. Helmsman, steer the ship!'

So the ship sailed merrily over the bright summer sea, among the islands and along the straits, until it came to the port of Laryma over against the long island of Euboea. Here Dionysus soon found new followers, and before long made his way to Orchomenus, a little to the north of Thebes, where Minyas was king. Here he stayed for some time, and all the people of the country were soon paying him divine honours and their vines were weighted to the ground with rich clusters of grapes.

The time drew near for him to continue on his way to the Cadmeia, for at length those of his followers from Nysa, a band of the inspired eastern women Bacchae, who had followed him from Thrace, at last overtook him.

But before he left Orchomenus a great celebration was held in his honour and the whole land made holiday. All except the three daughters of King Minyas who were jealous of the honours poured upon this stranger and insisted that he was an imposter and no son of Zeus.

So, while all the women of Orchomenus were dancing among the vines and running wild over the hills catching the smaller of the wild creatures and tearing them in their ecstasy, the three princesses sat at home and went on weaving a great tapestry of a leafy forest scene.

'Let these mad women worship this eastern stranger if they wish!' cried Alcathoe the eldest daugher. '*We* will show that Athena, the Lady of the Loom, is the goddess of our chief worship, and spend the day profitably while they desert their tasks and throng to this so-called festival.'

In vain Dionysus himself came to them in the form of a young girl and advised them to take part in the holy rites of Bacchus. He was forced to go to extreme measures. Suddenly the woven tapestry of green forest trees became green leaves indeed – and out of the great vine-hung trees which it had become poured a stream of nectar-scented wine which maddened them so, that to Alcathoe it seemed that Dionysus was a mad bull ready to charge her, to Leucippe he was a fierce lion, and to Aristippe he seemed a snarling leopard. In terror they fled into the green twilight of this enchanted wood – deeper and deeper, seeking to escape out of the light – twittering in their terror – twittering and waving their arms until

Jael Jordan

they were changed into bats, hanging with folded wings in the twilight under the high roof of the Castle of Orchomenus.

Next day Dionysus left Orchomenus, and wandered away with his band of Bacchae, round the western end of Lake Copais and across the plain by Coroneia and Thespiae until he came to Thebes – which was still only the fortified citadel known as the Cadmeia, though by now many houses were beginning to spring up outside the walls.

Otherwise there had been little change during the twenty years or so since the death of Semele. The wing of the palace in which she died had never been rebuilt, but still smouldered strangely even through the heaviest rains of winter. In spite of this, it was now generally believed that Semele had been killed by Zeus in punishment for pretending that her lover was not just a mortal adventurer but the Father of the Immortals himself. And no one was more eager to spread this tale than Pentheus the king.

Cadmus and Harmonia still lived, though long retired from any share in the government of the city. After the death or disappearance of all their other daughters, the one remaining, Agave, had become queen. Her husband was Echion, one of the Sown Men; and when he died their son Pentheus became king – setting aside the youngest of Cadmus and Harmonia's children, their only son, Polydorus, though by then he was almost of age to rule.

Pentheus was a proud and headstrong young man, obsessed with his own importance and sensitive to the slightest suggestion that anyone else might have a better claim to the throne than he. When he heard of the young man who had appeared in the neighbourhood of the Cadmeia declaring himself to be a new god called Dionysus or Bacchus, the son of Zeus and Semele, he reacted vigorously, declaring him to be an impostor and threatening death to any who believed in his divinity or observed his rites.

But these declarations did not prevent the Bacchic madness and ecstasy from falling upon most of the women of Thebes, and causing them to rush out of the city and over the foothills to Kithairon, with their skirts girt up short and ivy twined round their heads. For Dionysus was determined to prove his godhead in Thebes more surely than anywhere to wash away the false stain of dishonour from his mother's name.

Even more enraged, Pentheus sent his soldiers to scour the

country round about for the frienzied women – but in particular for Dionysus himself, whom they were commanded to catch and bind and bring a prisoner to the Cadmeia.

He had not long to wait, for within an hour the guard returned leading a tall, rather over-handsome young man, with flowing wine-dark hair crowned with a circle of vine leaves among which clustered both ripe grapes and vine-flowers – as if two seasons were combined in one.

'My Lord', said the Captain of the Guard, saluting Pentheus, 'here is the man you seek – if he is a man and not an Immortal. He was not difficult to catch; when we surrounded him he stood still and smiled at us, holding out his hands to be bound. But such women as we caught have all escaped from the prison: the ropes fell from their wrists, the doors flew open and they all fled up onto the mountain again, calling on their god "Bromios", or some such eastern name.'

At first Pentheus spoke his prisoner fair and caused the soldiers to unbind his hands – for he did not think that this youth could do any harm.

'Where do you come from? Who are you? and what is all this about a new god who has just come to Greece?'

'I come from Nysa and Tmolus, above Sardis', was the answer. 'Dionysus the son of Zeus initiated me into the mysteries of this new cult and I come to preach it in Greece so that all men and women may dance in his revels and worship him in that new ecstasy which his gift of wine brings with it.'

'Who and where is this Dionysus?' asked Pentheus.

'He is the divine son of Zeus and Semele', replied the captive, 'and he is with me now. If you can see me you can see him. And if you cannot see him it is because of your impiety and the hardness of your heart.'

When Pentheus heard this he became livid with fury.

'Seize him!' he cried to the guard. 'Bind him tightly and chain him with fetters of bronze in the palace stables. Let him see nothing but the gloom and smell nothing but the dung of the prison he deserves.'

'Pentheus, you do not realise what you are doing', said Dionysus solemnly. 'Think again. Think what and who you are – understand who and what I am!'

'I know that I am King of Thebes', shouted Pentheus. 'I am the sone of Agave and Echion, and my mother's father was Cadmus who wedded Harmonia, the daughter of two Immortals, Ares and Aphrodite. As for you – well, we shall see if you are still so impudent after a few days of eating oats with the horses. As for these loose women of yours, and any of our own who have been misled by them – well, any we catch we'll sell into slavery: that will soon stop them from running wild on the mountain!'

'I go', answered Dionysus. 'I can do no more than fulfil my destiny. But be sure: Dionysus whom you deny and insult will exact full payment for this outrage. When you put *me* in bonds you put *him* in bonds. The Immortals do not suffer such insults lightly.'

Dionysus was led away and fettered hand and foot in the darkest corner of the royal stables. And as night drew in over the Cadmeia, Pentheus rejoiced in his victory.

But there was one in Thebes who knew better than he – and did not rejoice. This was the blind seer Teiresias, the wisest and greatest of all mortal prophets. And he made haste to visit Pentheus, with the aged white-haired Cadmus, to seek to dissuade him from his mad course.

Teiresias, the greatest of all prophets of Ancient Greece – both in his lifetime and after his death when Odysseus called him up from the Underworld, had a strange history. He was the son or grandson of Udaeus, one of the Sown Men, and of the nymph Chariclo, best loved attendant of Athena, the Goddess of Wisdom. When he was a boy and but just beginning to study the Seer's art, he had a strange experience with the Sacred Snakes on Mount Helicon beyond Kithairon where the Muses dwelt, and was turned into a woman. A year later he met the Sacred Serpents again and was changed back into a man. While still wandering in a daze, scarce knowing what he was, he had the misfortune to come upon Athena and his own mother Chariclo bathing in the Fountain of Hippocrene on Helicon.

'Alas!' cried Athena when she saw him, 'what jealous god, son of Chariclo, has led you here to see what no man may see? Be it the last thing your mortal eyes ever look upon!'

By rights Teiresias should have died for what he had seen, even as Actaeon died. But as what he had done was by the purest chance, Athena merely took away his sight. And when Chariclo knelt at her feet with bitter tears begging for her son's pardon, she said:

'I cannot undo what I have done, for such is the law of the Immortals – and it is also the law that blindness or, more usually, death, shall fall upon any mortal who beholds any of the Immortals when that god does not choose it. But in token of my love for you I here and now bestow on your son the gift of prophecy. He shall understand the speech of bird and beast even as Melampus did; and he shall read the future and the past, what is before him and what is far away, more surely even than prophets which are to be – Polyidus and Chalcas, Cassandra and Laocoon and his own daughter Manto. And moreover another gift shall be his at the hands of Zeus which I know but may not speak now...'

And indeed scarcely a year had passed before Zeus and Hera quarrelled as to whether the husband or the wife knows greater pleasure in the high delights of marriage. Knowing that he alone of mortals and immortals had been both male and female, they turned naturally to Teiresias for judgment. And Teiresias answered:

'If in ten parts love's joys be split – why then, man enjoys one part of the woman's ten.'

This so angered Hera that she cursed Teiresias with blindness – forgetting that he was blind already. But Zeus laughed, saying:

'Teiresias, you true prophet however blind you may be – I give you a life equal in length to the natural lives of three ordinary men.'

And this came to pass: for Teiresias, born when Cadmus still ruled over Thebes, died only when Thersander, the great-great-great-great-grandson of Cadmus was King of Thebes more than two hundred years later.

Though still relatively young, Teiresias was already a venerable prophet of great fame when he came to Pentheus to warn him against his treatment of Dionysus. But even Teiresias, backed by old Cadmus himself, could not make him change his mind.

'Dear grandson, be guided by Teiresias', begged Cadmus. 'Remember what happened to Actaeon and have a care that you do not earn the enmity of another Immortal. And even if Dionysus is not a god, it is surely better that the people should believe him to be one and so bring honour rather than disgrace upon the memory of Semele.'

'Don't presume to teach me!' shouted Pentheus. 'I say this man is an impostor – and I know how to deal with any man who pretends to be a god and leads the women of my city astray as he and his followers are doing. Such as he deserve to die, and die he shall; stoned to death before all the people here in the Cadmeia.'

'Poor wretch, how little you know what you are saying', said Teiresias. 'If you continue in this mind you will bring upon yourself a worse fate than befell Actaeon. Come Cadmus, let us set ivy wreaths on our heads and go to entreat the gods to spare your grandson, mad though he be. Let us pray, for the city's sake, that evil may not fall on us all.'

But it seemed that their prayers were vain, for scarcely had the old man and the prophet gone down from the Cadmeia when there came a peal of thunder, and the lightning struck down re-kindling the blaze that had never quite gone out in the shell of that part of the palace where Semele had met her fate. Then the ground shook and heaved with earthquake, and the royal stables crashed in ruins to the ground. Once more the lightning flashed, filling the palace with flame until it seemed for a moment as if it were all on fire. The thunder rumbled away in the distance, and the Stranger who was Dionysus appeared walking calmly from the ruins.

'This is intolerable', cried Pentheus. 'How have you escaped? And how dare you come before me as if you feared nothing?'

'Dionysus freed me from my bonds', was the answer. 'And Dionysus does not fear to come before any earthly king. But before you speak, hear what this herdsman has to say whom I see hurrying hither from the hills. I know what he comes to tell; but when you hear it you will seek my aid instead of my death.'

Even as he spoke one of the royal herdsmen came running into the courtyard, knelt before Pentheus and began to pour out a strange tale.

It seemed that while he was guarding the king's herd of cattle in a valley among the foothills of Kithairon he had seen the women of Thebes, headed by Agave, performing the rites of Dionysus. There were young women and old, all filled with an ecstasy that gave them supernatural strength. Their hair was flying loose and they were clad in fawn skins over their short skirts – all without fear. Most of them carried a thyrsus – a long thin staff crowned with a pine cone, the symbol of Dionysus-worship – and with these they seemed able to perform miracles. One would strike a rock and a rivulet of milk would gush out; some would turn a pool of water into wine at a touch; while for others the very thyrsus would drip great gouts of golden honey. Now they would rest on the hillside; now they would dash through the woods waving their thyrsi and uttering loud cries of adoration for their new god: 'Bacchus! Evoi! Bromios! Saboi!'

The herdsman had gone in haste to find the other herdsmen of Thebes and together they had tried to catch Agave to bring back with them to the king. But when they saw them, the Bacchae had attacked them, led by Agave herself shrieking: 'We are being hunted by these men! Follow me with your wands for weapons!'

Then the herdsmen had fled, and the women attacked the cattle as if in mistake for them, the thyrsi cutting like spears, while several of the calves were seized and torn to pieces with naked hands.

'Women defeating men? Only because a god possessed them', ended the herdsmen. 'When we and the cattle were defeated and driven away the women went to a spring which gushed out at the touch of a thyrsus, and washed away the blood from their hands and faces... My advice to you, lord king, is that you welcome this new god into your city. He is very powerful. And he is giving us all this wonderful new gift of wine. Surely if *he* is not a god, then Aphrodite who gives us the ecstasies of love is no goddess either.'

'This madness is like a spreading fire!' cried Pentheus. 'I will have to call up the whole army to bring these women to their senses...'

'Pentheus', interrupted the Stranger with a sudden authority that calmed the king's anger for a moment. 'Listen to me. Do not take up arms against a god. He will never allow you to drive his Bacchae from their revels, however large an army you bring against them. My advice is that you bow down and worship this Dionysus – a man cannot fight against a god.'

'I'll make a sacrifice indeed!' cried Pentheus. 'First you, and then the ringleaders among these women – yes, even if one of them is my own mother –'

'Pentheus!' the clear, quiet tones numbed him. 'Listen to me. If you will not be warned, then let me guide you to where these women are so that you can see for yourself whether what they are doing is evil or not.'

'Yes! Yes!' said Pentheus, suddenly changing his mind as if a spell had been cast upon him. 'I desire to see these women more than anything in the world. I would give much fine gold if I could look upon their revels and remain myself unseen.'

'That you shall do', came the answer. 'You must dress yourself as a woman – as one of the Bacchae yourself – and then I will lead you to Kithairon and show you how you may spy upon them and take no harm if you are discovered.'

Pentheus was more eager than ever at this. And very soon he was dressed up in an embroidered robe, with a snood round his head and vine leaves in his hair. As he put on these clothes the Bacchic influence took possession of him more and more strongly.

'I can see two suns in the sky and a double Cadmeia', he cried excitedly. 'And a bull is leading me – you stranger, you seem to have turned into a bull, with horns growing on your head. Were you ever an animal? You certainly have the look of a bull.'

'The god is our escort', was the answer. 'He was hostile before, but now you have made your peace with him you see him as you should – in one of his many shapes. Come now to Kithairon: there you will find the Bacchae and may spy on all that they do.'

'Yes', agreed Pentheus as he followed his strange guide out of the palace courtyard. 'Yes, I'll spy all right; I'll climb into a tree and watch all their secrets, their rites and mysteries that no man should see.'

Dionysus led Pentheus up the mountain, while two guards followed some distance behind. At length they came to the edge of a grassy glade and saw, beyond a steep ravine, where pines stood dark beside the waters of a mountain stream, the Bacchae sitting resting beneath the trees. Some of them were twisting fresh wreaths for their heads or tresses of ivy to wind round their thyrsi, while others were singing in praise of Dionysus.

'I cannot see them clearly enough', whispered Pentheus. 'It would be better if I climbed a tree –'

Even as he spoke, Dionysus stretched out his hand in which he too now held a thyrsus and moved it slowly down. And, as if in obedience to his gesture, a tall fir bowed down before him until it was bent like an arch, with its top brushing the ground at the feet of Dionysus.

'Take hold', he said to Pentheus, who clutched the top of the tree, which at once rose into the air until it stood upright again with him perched near its very top.

Then Dionysus cried in a great voice that seemed to come from every direction at once: 'My women, I Dionysus bring you the man who mocked you and ridiculed me and my sacred rites. Take vengeance upon him as it is ordained.'

For a moment there was a silence as if all nature held its breath. Then with wild cries the Bacchae rushed down to the stream, crossed it leaping from boulder to boulder like mountain goats, led by Agave. They found Pentheus easily enough, but at first could not dislodge him from his tree. They began by pelting him with stones, but the tree was too high; and as there were no branches for most of the trunk they would not climb to him. He sat high above their eager, ravening reach, a pitiful and miserable captive: for now the madness had left him suddenly, leaving him up a tree in a ridiculous costume and, as he was only too well aware, in great danger. The worst thing of all was that the maddened women were led by his own mother Agave – who did not know him.

It was she who now bade the women bring oak branches to use as crowbars to pry up the roots of the tree. When they had loosened it as much as they could, Agave shouted:

'Come women, stand round in a circle and take hold of the trunk. We will either pull it down or shake to the ground the wild beast who is treed here. If we do not get him, he will tell the secrets of our mystic dance and the other mysteries of Dionysus to all the world.'

In their ecstasy their strength was so great that at length they brought the tree crashing to the ground. Bruised and bleeding Pentheus extracted himself from the twisted branches and, throwing off his disguise until he was almost naked, flung himself at Agave's feet, crying:

'Mother, what are you doing? I am Pentheus – I am your own, your only son – Pentheus whom you bore in the house of Echion my father and your husband. Pity me, spare me – do not kill me for what I have done in my foolish pride!'

But Agave was foaming at the mouth with the wild ecstasy of Dionysus that possessed her, and she did not know him. She cried out that it was a lion who was attacking them, and seized hold of Pentheus by the arm, wrenching it away at the shoulder. Then the other maddened women closed in and tore him to pieces.

When the terrible deed was done, Agave set off for Thebes with the other women following behind, holding the head of Pentheus proudly before her and still thinking that it was a lion they had killed.

When they got back to the Cadmeia, Agave called for her father Cadmus, and the old man came out of the palace in fear of his life – for the two guards had got back to Thebes before the women and told him what had happened on Kithairon.

At first Agave insisted that she had killed a young lion and brought its head back as a trophy. But very soon, as her Bacchic madness died away, she realised what she had done, and her grief and horror were bitter indeed.

While she was thinking of killing herself – for suicide was no sin among the ancient Greeks, but an acceptable means either of self-punishment or of escape from miseries or difficulties too hard to bear – Dionysus appeared once more in the Cadmeia and spoke comforting words to both Agave and Cadmus.

'What was fated has befallen', said Dionysus. 'You, Agave, and your sisters spread false and malicious rumours about my mother Semele, and so brought inevitable punishment upon yourselves. Pentheus too sought his own doom by persecuting me and my disciples. But now the doom is ended, except that you Agave must go out into exile. And Cadmus and Harmonia must go too, as was decreed from the beginning. They shall found a new kingdom in the far north of Greece, and be turned into serpents – and at length come to eternal life and happiness in the Elysian Fields, the Islands of the Blessed.'

And it fell out even as Dionysus had said. Cadmus, Harmonia and Agave set out with a few faithful followers and after a long journey in a cart drawn by bullocks they came to the land of Illyria, which is now called Albania. Here Cadmus helped one section of the people to conquer and rule the rest, and himself became their king for a short while, and is even said to have had a son called Illyrius who gave his name to the country, which had before been called Enchelea. Agave too married again, a minor king called Lycothenes: but she was doomed to be unlucky in her loves, and brought him to his death in the Illyrian war, after which Cadmus ruled his country too until the day came when he began his penance as a snake for having slain the Dragon of Ares long ago when he first came to the site of Thebes that was to be.

But meanwhile Dionysus went on his triumphant way through

Greece, having many adventures as he brought the gift of wine to city after city – to Athens and to Sparta, and last of all to Argos.

In Argolis he fought with the great hero Perseus and was mortally wounded. And, as he was not yet quite a god, this wound brought him down to the Realm of the Dead where Hades reigns. But when he had crossed the River Styx and come to the meeting place of Acheron, river of wailing, and Lethe, river of forgetfulness, he stood before Hades and his pale bride Persephone, and said:

'King of the Dead, by the will of Zeus, who is my father. I do not remain here as your subject, but rise presently through the earth and take my place with the other Immortals. But it is my wish to take Semele, my mother, with me. I beg of you to release her from death so that she can accompany me.'

'That may not be', answered Hades, 'unless you give me, in exchange for your mother, your best beloved who now lives upon the earth.'

'I will do just that', cried Dionysus gaily. 'Ampelos is my best beloved. See! Here he lives again!' As he spoke he struck his thyrsus into the barren ground, and at once it took root, sent out leaves, and grew great clusters of grapes.

Hades nodded and smiled – glad that his dark kingdom should now be possessed of so choice a gift as the means of making wine. And at his command Semele was set free.

Then Zeus, who had been watching all, opened a chasm in the earth through which Dionysus passed leading Semele by the hand. And in Olympus she was received by all the Immortals under the new name of Thyone. And even Hera greeted her kindly and forgot her jealousy.

But over that deep chasm in Hermione which leads straight to the land of the dead no bird dares fly even to this day.

VI

AMPHION AND ZETHUS

After the death of Pentheus and the departure of Cadmus and Harmonia to Illyria, Polydorus, their youngest child, became King of Thebes, being now of age and a far better claimant than Thalus the only son of Pentheus. Polydorus married Nycteis, daughter of a certain Nycteus whose father was Chthonius, one of the Sown Men. They had one son called Labdacus, and when his father died soon after his birth, Lycus the brother of Nycteus, made himself regent until Labdacus should come of age. When this happened Lycus duly gave back the throne to him. But Labdacus also died young, leaving only a single heir, Laius, and Lycus slipped back onto the throne and this time proclaimed himself king. While he was still only regent it chanced that Zeus visited the Cadmeia once more in the guise of a lover, his beloved this time being Antiope the daughter of Nycteus, the fame of whose beauty had spread through all Greece.

Now it chanced that Epopeus, the King of Sicyon, a city not far from Corinth that looks north across the Gulf of Helicon and Boeotia, had already fallen in love with her. Lycus and Nycteus had both refused to let him marry her, having thoughts of some far more important king as her husband; but Antiope herself had fallen in love with Epopeus – and it is indeed probable that Zeus had taken on his shape when visiting her.

Certain it is that Antiope sent for help to Epopeus, knowing that in his rage Lycus might well have her stoned to death when he discovered what was happening – and that her story of a divine lover would no more be believed in Thebes than Semele's had been.

Epopeus, however, not only believed her story but proved the depth of his love by carrying her away to Sicyon and marrying her.

But Lycus and Nycteus gathered an army and marched over the mountains and across the Isthmus of Corinth to attack Sicyon. A great battle was fought in which the Thebans were defeated and returned to the Cadmeia carrying both Lycus and Nycteus sorely wounded. Lycus soon recovered, but Nycteus was fatally hurt, and it was soon obvious that he was dying.

Accordingly he sent for his brother and said: 'Lycus, this must not go unavenged. Swear to me now that you will attack Sicyon again, kill Epopeus, and bring back my daughter. When all this is forgotten you may still find some great king to be her husband.'

Lycus swore that; and when he was sufficiently recovered from his own wound, and Nycteus had died and been buried as became a Theban warrior descended from a Sown Man, he gathered an army together and set out for Sicyon.

Meanwhile Epopeus had returned to Sicyon with his victorious army and begun to build a temple to Pallas Athena in honour of his victory. And when it was finished he prayed to the goddess to give him some sign by which he would know whether it was built and decorated to her liking and if it found favour in her eyes. And in token of her approval Athena caused a stream of pure olive oil to flow out of the temple door: for the olive tree was sacred to her and she had planted the first one on the Acropolis at Athens.

But Epopeus had also been wounded in the battle, and in his eagerness to build the temple he had neglected his wound. Now it broke out again and festered, so that he died.

Lycus was already marching from Thebes with his new army. But when they came before the city of Sicyon, they were met by the new king Lamedon who made a lasting peace between the two cities, handing over Antiope to Lycus and with her a fine in gold to atone for what Epopeus had done.

So the army marched to Boeotia, going by the Isthmus and over the mountains of Megara to Aegosthena and thence up the long sloping valley to Eleutherai at the pass over Mount Kithairon which leads down to Thebes.

And here at Eleutherai twin sons were born to Antiope – and, by order of Lycus, they were left to die on the slopes of Kithairon. But Antiope was taken back to Thebes, and there she was made the slave of Dirce, the cruel, ambitious wife of Lycus. For twenty years she suffered this cruel bondage, until the appointed time came. Then

Zeus caused the palace doors to open silently at dead of night and, unseen even by her, he led Antiope out, and away through the foothills of Kithairon until in the dawning she came to the mountain itself.

All day she toiled up the steep slopes, and in the evening came to a herdsman's cottage in a fold of the mountain, where two young shepherds welcomed her with the traditional hospitality of Greece where from then until now there has only been one word for both 'stranger' and 'guest'.

Now, Zeus had seen to it that no harm came to his twin sons exposed on Kithairon by command of cruel Lycus to die of cold or be eaten by wild beasts. They had not been left for very long when they were found by a herdsman whose own baby sons had just died. He carried them home to his wife, and the couple adopted the foundlings and brought them up as their own children, naming them Amphion and Zethus.

Fron the beginning, however, the two boys showed that they were no herdsman's sons, growing up to be handsome young men divinely gifted – Amphion in the music of the lyre, and Zethus in the more practical things of life such as the use of arms and the arts of a warrior and a huntsman. And for this Zethus rather looked down on his brother – and indeed their differences once led to a quarrel: for Zethus said that to play the lyre, to sing and to make up poetry was a mere waste of time and unpatriotic at that since the minstrel was of no use to his city, while the warrior could defend it, the mason could build it, and the farmer could feed it.

They were both tending their flock of sheep when Antiope found them: Amphion keeping them happily together by the music of his lyre, while Zethus guarded them from ravening wolves. Neither of them had any more idea that Antiope was their mother than she had that they were her sons. In fact, thinking she was merely an escaped slave from some Boeotian village, they refused to let her enter their cottage or to protect her from any who might pursue her.

Before long, Dirce arrived at Eleutherai in search of Antiope accompanied by a group of women who were arrayed like the Bacchae – and indeed they had all been celebrating the rites of Dionysus on Kithairon. Not knowing who she was, Amphion and Zethus gave up Antiope to Dirce, who set out triumphantly for the Cadmeia with her captive.

But scarcely were they gone when the old herdsman who had

found and adopted Amphion and Zethus came rushing up to them exclaiming:

'My sons, you are likely to be in great trouble. You must at once make sacrifice to the Furies.'

'Why to the Furies?' asked Amphion.

'Because Zeus has revealed to me that it was your mother, Antiope, whom you refused to protect', was the answer. 'You have given her over to Dirce, that savage aunt of her's, who will surely torture her and put her to death.'

As soon as they had heard all the story from their foster-father, Amphion and Zethus set out in hot haste after Antiope and her captors. They overtook them just before they reached the Cadmeia; and when Antiope told them all that she had suffered, they took Dirce and tied her by the hair to the horns of a wild bull, which soon tore her in pieces.

The two brothers then hastened back to Eleutherai, taking their mother with them. But Lycus was already in pursuit of Antiope, and very soon the two young men saw him approaching with a band of armed soldiers.

'There is no way of escape from these men!' exclaimed Amphion bitterly. 'If Zeus is indeed our father, he should rescue us and help us to punish Lycus. But we cannot escape the punishment for shedding Dirce's blood. If we wait here we are certain to be killed as we are so greatly outnumbered.'

'Hide in the hut – I'll see what I can do', said the old herdsman. 'But have your swords ready in case I can persuade Lycus to come in.'

So Amphion and Zethus hid in the cottage with Antiope, while the herdsman remained outside to face Lycus, who came storming up the hill with drawn sword, crying:

'Where is Antiope? She had escaped me! Have you seen her? Do you know where she is hiding?'

'She is in my hut here', answered the herdsman. 'My two sons found her wandering on the mountain side and brought her here.'

'Then I will slay her with my own hand!' said Lycus grimly. 'She'll soon find that the gods who used to love her, as she idly boasted, are but feeble comrades in arms!'

So saying, he rushed into the hut with drawn sword. But there Amphion and Zethus sprang upon him, disarmed him, and dragged him out to kill.

Jael Jordan

But as they were about to slay him, Hermes the Messenger of Zeus appeared suddenly and stayed their hands:

'Stop, King Amphion!' he cried. 'Stop, I command you. I, Hermes, come from Zeus to make plain all that was hidden. Lycus, you must give up your crown and go into exile. Your wife Dirce has met her just doom – tied to the horns of a bull and torn in pieces. Go first and gather her remains: burn them on a pyre as the custom is, and then scatter her ashes in the Spring of Ares behind the Cadmeia, where Cadmus fought the Dragon. In memory of her that fountain and the stream which gushes from it shall ever more be called after her – the Fountain of Dirce. As for these two young men, learn Lycus and all you his followers that they are Amphion and Zethus, the sons which Antiope bore to Zeus himself. They are the rightful rulers of the Cadmeia and all the lands which shall soon be called Thebes. For they are commanded to build a wall with seven gates round the city which is already springing up beneath the Cadmeia.

'Amphion and Zethus, when you have built the city you shall marry: one of you Niobe the daughter of Tantalus of Phrygia, and the other the maiden Thebe born of the race of the Sown Men: and after her the city shall be called Thebes for ever more. Now make all speed – for these are the commands which Zeus has sent you.'

Then Hermes returned to Olympus. But Lycus led Antiope, Amphion and Zethus to the Cadmeia with all honour. And when the funeral rites for Dirce were completed he handed over the Crown to Amphion and went away into exile.

After this Amphion and Zethus became the Kings of Thebes – for Laius the rightful king was too young to rule, and was taken away secretly from Thebes for safety and sent to dwell with Pelops, King of Elis.

But Amphion and Zethus began at once to build a great wall with seven gates around Thebes, hewing the stones from a neighbouring hill and having them piled at the sites of these gates.

'Now', said Amphion to his brother, remembering their ancient quarrel, 'let us see whether you the strong, athletic man, or I, the musician and dreamer, can best help in the building of Thebes!'

Stung by this, Zethus began lifting great masses of stone and carrying them to their appointed places in the walls. But very soon his strength gave out and he sank exhausted to the ground.

Then Amphion tuned his lyre and began to play a wondrous harmony which Hermes had taught him. And, to the sound of his lyre, the stones moved into place of themselves – more and more and more of them until they darkened the midday sun like a flight of locusts. And so in one day the City of Thebes was surrounded with a great wall pierced by seven gates – and music triumphed over brute strength.

To please Zethus, who was rather disgruntled, Amphion named the city Thebes after his wife Thebe. But it seems that Thebe died soon, for Zethus then took to wife Aedon the daughter of Pandareus of Miletus in Asia Minor. And Amphion also took a wife from Asia, Niobe the daughter of Tantalus of Smyrna – that same Tantalus who betrayed the secrets of Zeus and was punished after his death by being chained up to the chin in water which always moved away as he stooped to drink.

As King of Thebes, Amphion became owner of the fatal Necklace of Harmonia which he gave to Niobe who was ridiculously vain of her beauty and her noble family. She bore Amphion seven sons and seven daughters, and was for ever boasting about the size of her family and their remarkable good looks.

This nearly drove poor Aedon the wife of Zethus out of her wits. For she had only one son Itylus and one daughter Neis, and she was terribly jealous of Niobe. So jealous did she become at length that she decided to murder Amyclas, Niobe's eldest son.

Now it chanced that on the evening when she determined to carry out her evil purpose, Amyclas and Itylus had been playing together and, as the game of the moment demanded each was pretending to be the other, they had even changed clothes and were sleeping in each other's bed. So that, when the half-crazed Aedon crept in at dead of night and stabbed the sleeping child, it was her own son Itylus that she murdered and not Amyclas as she had intended.

When morning came and she knew what she had done, poor Aedon became quite mad. With long, mournful cries of woe she fled out of Thebes and away into the thickets of Kithairon. All day she ran, and as night fell the Immortals took pity on her and turned her into the first nightingale: and all nightingales after her still cry by night 'Itylus! Itylus! Itylus!'

After the lucky escape of her son Amyclas, Niobe became even more outrageously vain, and began likening herself to the Immortals themselves.

But such pride could only bring the wrath of the gods upon her and the judgment of the goddess Nemesis. And vengeance came on the day of the feast in honour of Leto, the divine mother of Apollo and Artemis. On that day the priestess Manto, daughter of the prophet blind Teiresias, went through the streets of Thebes proclaiming:

'Women of Thebes, come thronging to Leto's temple and give to her and to her children twain incense and pious prayer, wreathing your heads with ivy. By my mouth Leto speaks.'

But scarcely had she passed into the temple when Niobe came up to it, stood upon the steps and cried:

'What madness is this, to prefer the gods of whom you have only heard to those whom you can see? Why is Leto worshipped on this day while my divinity still goes unrecognised? Do you not realise that I am the daughter of Tantalus – of the only mortal who has ever sat at the table of the Immortals on Olympus? Moreover I have Atlas the Titan for one grandfather and Zeus himself for the other! In Phrygia where my father reigns I would be receiving divine honours. And what is this Leto compared with me? She is the daughter of a Titan, that is all. Once the whole earth refused her a resting place and she was forced at length to seek shelter on the little floating island of Delos. And there she bore children – yes, just one son and one daughter. While look at me, the mother of seven sons and seven daughters. I am the beloved of good fortune – far happier and more blessed than Leto. It is *me* you should worship, not her.'

Such blasphemy as this was too much for Leto who turned at once to Apollo and Artemis and bade them avenge her wrongs and prove her divinity and their's. And so they strung their bows and set arrows to the strings – the terrible arrows of pestilence which it is their duty to discharge when Zeus bids them visit mortals with a plague for their misdoings. And they shot down six of the seven sons of Niobe and Amphion and six of the seven daughters, leaving only Amyclas and Chloris; and Amyclas ran mad and was lost to Thebes as surely as if he had been stricken dead like his brothers.

It is said that Amyclas was later cured of his madness and, far away in the south of Greece, became the father of a beautiful daughter called Daphne. She vowed ever to remain unwed and to follow Artemis in the chase. She gathered together a band of maidens like-minded with herself, and soon they became famous from Elis to Laconia – not least for the great beauty of their leader Daphne. Indeed she was so beautiful that she had the misfortune to inspire love both in the mortal prince Leucippus of Elis and in the Immortal Apollo. Her mortal lover disguised himself as a woman and joined Daphne's troop of huntresses, where he soon became her favourite companion. This made Apollo jealous, and one day when they were near a river he suddenly put into Daphne's mind a great desire to bathe. As they began to take off their clothes they saw that Leucippus was unwilling to follow their example; they therefore tore his clothes from him, and when they thus became aware of the deceit he had practised and the plot he had devised, they all plunged their spears into his body. All except Daphne who was already falling in love with him: but even as she realised this she saw Apollo advancing towards her. She fled at once with the Immortal after her; and when she saw that she must be overtaken she implored Zeus to save her and he turned her into the first laurel tree, now called *Daphne Laureola.*

The only other child of Amphion and Niobe to escape was Chloris, and she lived to become the wife of Neleus, King of Pylos, and the mother of Nestor – the oldest and wisest of the heroes who fought at Troy.

As for Niobe she was quite inconsolable for the tragedy which had befallen her. She left Thebes and set out for Smyrna, her birthplace. And, weeping ever weeping, she wandered over the world until she reached her first home. And even then she could not rest but wandered, ever weeping, on Mount Siphylos, until Zeus took pity on her and turned her into a stone which you may still see weeping to this day.

After all these tragedies Amphion too went a little mad. Blaming Apollo for all that had happened, he set out for Delphi, seeking vengeance. When he got to Delphi he attacked the Temple as if it were a hostile city, but was suddenly slain by one of Apollo's arrows. He was carried back to Thebes and buried in the same tomb as his brother Zethus who had died of grief.

Even Antiope did not escape the vengeance decreed by angry Leto – though some say that in her case it was the vengeance of

Dionysus for the fate she had brought upon his faithful worshipper Dirce. Certain it is that she too ran mad and wandered all over Greece, until Phocus the King of Tithorea cured her and made her his wife.

When Phocus and Antiope died they were buried under a high mound of earth at Tithorea. Soon a strange superstition grew which was believed for hundreds of years: if a man of Tithorea could steal earth from the grave of Amphion and Zethus, and sprinkle it on the grave of Phocus and Antiope, in early May when the constellation of Taurus is in the ascendant, their crops would be good. But in Thebes they believed that if earth were stolen from the grave during that time some disaster would befall the city. And so each year there was a great contest, the young men of Thebes striving to guard the grave from the young men of Tithorea who were trying to steal earth from it.

VII

THE MISFORTUNES OF OEDIPUS

When Amphion seized the throne of Thebes the rightful king, Laius the son of Labdacus, who was only a child, was smuggled out of the Cadmeia and sent to Elis to be protected by its king, Pelops the brother of Niobe.

Here Laius grew up safely and became a skilled charioteer. So skilful was he that Pelops entrusted his favourite son, Chrysippus, to him to instruct in the art. But this led to trouble, for Laius developed a passion for the boy and finally carried him off to Thebes by force after they had been competing in a chariot race.

This was when Laius had been recalled to be King of Thebes after the death of Amphion, and so he was able to defy Pelops who sent an embassy led by his two sons Atreus and Thyestes. With them came their mother Hippodameia who was bent on getting rid of Chrysippus: for Chrysippus was not her son, his mother being the nymph Astyoche, and she was jealous on her own sons' account since Pelops preferred him to them and wished to make him his successor.

Hippodameia began by trying to persuade Atreus and Thyestas to murder Chrysippus by throwing him down a well. But they refused since both they and Chrysippus were Laius's guests, and to kill a fellow-guest was a sin against the laws of hospitality.

Accordingly Hippodameia decided to kill Chrysippus herself and get rid of Laius at the same time by making it appear that he was the murderer. Accordingly she crept into their bedroom at dead of night and plunged Laius's sword through the body of his bed-fellow. But Chrysippus lived long enough to convince Atreus and Thyestes that Hippodameia had killed him, not Laius. She fled to Argolis when her crime was discovered, and Pelops recalled Atreus and

Thyestes to Elis, having decided not to pursue the quarrel with Laius now that Chrysippus was dead by his wife's hand. But he laid a curse on Laius and all his descendants for three generations to come – that they should live in fear and die unnaturally.

Laius was now King of Thebes, and he proposed to marry his cousin Jocasta, the grand-daughter of Pentheus, a young and beautiful girl. But before doing so he made the journey to Delphi to consult the Oracle of Apollo about the curse which Pelops had laid on him and his house. And the god replied clearly and positively through the lips of his priestess, the Pythia:

'King Laius, for your sin against Chrysippus, and the evil thing you have brought into Greece, this fate is laid upon you: you must not have a son – for if you do he will kill you, which would be a crime in the eyes of gods and men, and he will marry his own mother – which would be a greater pollution still. But if you have no son, the curse will die with you.'

After hearing this, a wiser and more temperate man would not have married. But Laius was now besotted with the beauty of the girl Jocasta, as he had been with the boy Chrysippus – and he not only married her and made her his Queen, but he gave her the fatal Necklace of Harmonia which brought no luck to any who wore it.

In due time a son was born to Jocasta and Laius. But, mindful of the Oracle, Laius pierced the baby's feet, shackled them and gave him to a herdsman to expose on Kithairon to die of cold and be eaten by wolves or vultures.

After this he saw to it that Jocasta had no further children, and they lived happily enough together for more than twenty years.

But then a strange and terrible plague came to bring woe to Thebes. It came in the form of a creature called the Sphinx. She had the head and breasts of a woman, the body and claws of a lion and the wings of a great eagle, and she took up her abode on Mount Phikion, a rocky hillock near Thebes. Hera had sent her to punish the Thebans for not banishing Laius on account of the abduction of Chrysippus, and the Sphinx laid waste the fields and killed the flocks and herds; nor would she leave the land until someone could answer a riddle which she asked all those who came against her. And all those who could not solve the riddle she flung to their death down the steep cliff above which she sat, and then tore them to pieces and ate them.

Jael Jordan

When it became obvious that none of the Thebans could answer the riddle, Laius set out in his chariot with a few followers to consult the Oracle at Delphi. But he never came back; and only one attendant was able to return to Thebes, where he gave out that Laius had been set on and killed by a band of robbers in the Narrow Way of Schiste where the road from Daulis meets the roads from Thebes and Delphi.

As Laius was dead, without a son to succeed him, his wife's brother Creon took the throne, and proved himself a good and wise ruler. But he could not save his country from the Sphinx; and when his own eldest son Haemon had been killed by the monster, he declared that anyone who could deal with the Sphinx should marry Jocasta and become King of Thebes.

Princes in search of a fortune came eagerly to Thebes; but all in vain, until a young man called Oedipus, who said that he was the son of Polybus, King of Corinth, (the grandson of Epopeus of Sicyon who had been Antiope's first husband) arrived to try his fortune.

Up to Mount Phikion he went and boldly shouted defiance to the Sphinx, bidding her either leave Thebes in peace or fight with him.

'If you can answer my riddle rightly, I will go of my own free will', said the Sphinx smiling sweetly with her woman's mouth – but unsheathing her lion's claws from her pads as she spoke.

'Ask!' cried Oedipus, and the Sphinx replied:

'What is that which has one voice and yet becomes four-footed in the morning and two footed at noon and three-footed in the evening?'

Then Oedipus answered with a cry of triumph: 'A Man! For in the morning of his life he crawls upon all fours as a baby; in the noontide of life he walks upon two feet as a warrior should; but in the evening of his days he uses a stick as his third leg!'

When the Sphinx heard her riddle answered correctly she was seized with such a frenzy of rage that she fell off her rock over the cliff edge, and – her wings notwithstanding – she was as surely killed by the fall as Haemon and the others had been.

The Sphinx being dead Oedipus claimed the reward, which Creon honourably handed over to him. And so Oedipus married Jocasta and became King of Thebes. And in course of time they had four children: their daughters Antigone and Ismene, and two sons Polynices and Eteocles.

For many years Oedipus reigned well and happily over Thebes, much helped by his handsome wife Jocasta and his wise brother-in-law Creon. But about the time that his eldest child Antigone was just growing up, with the other three still only children, a fresh curse fell upon Thebes.

This time it was only a pestilence; and after many had died and no means of stopping it could be found, Oedipus decided that it must be some punishment sent by the gods; and he dispatched Creon to Delphi to consult the Oracle.

Creon returned with a very satisfactory answer from Apollo: the murderer of Laius was still at liberty and living in Thebes; the pestilence would stop if he were killed or driven out of the city.

On hearing this, Oedipus called the people together and begged the killer to give himself up; and he promised to let him go free so long as he left Thebes and never again crossed the borders of Boeotia. But when no one came forward either to admit the deed or accuse someone else of it, Oedipus sent for the blind prophet Teiresias and urged him to tell by his arts who the killer of Laius was.

Teiresias seemed so unwilling to speak that Oedipus jumped to the conclusion that he must have been one in a plot to kill King Laius.

'If you are mad enough to think such a thing', exclaimed Teiresias, 'I will tell you the real truth of the matter. It is *you* who must go forth as an exile from Thebes, for *you* are the accursed defiler of this land!'

At this Oedipus flew into one of his violent rages and accused Teiresias of being in league with Creon to have him driven from Thebes so that Creon could take the throne.

'I tell you', answered Teiresias solemnly, 'that the murderer of Laius is here before me, in seeming an alien but soon to be found a Theban – which discovery will bring him little joy. A blind man who now has sight, a beggar who now is rich, he shall wander in strange lands feeling the ground before him with his staff – as I do.'

This only enraged Oedipus more, and he accused Creon to his face of plotting with Teiresias to gain him the throne.

'But why should I want it?' asked Creon in bewilderment. 'As your brother-in-law I enjoy all that you and Jocasta have without any of the cares of kingship. I should be mad to envy you your place – let alone try to take it.'

Oedipus, however, was not convinced. He gave up his first idea of executing or exiling Creon, but he placed him under house-arrest, and went to tell Jocasta what had happened.

When she heard what Teiresias had said, she laughed bitterly and exclaimed:

'My dear lord, you may put from your mind all this nonsense that is gleaned from seers and oracles. I will prove it to you. An oracle came to Laius once – I will not say from Apollo, but at least from his Oracle – that he was doomed to be killed by his own child, sprung from him and me. Now Laius, as we all know, was murdered one day at a place where three roads meet by foreign robbers. And our only child was not three days old when Laius, mindful of the prophecy, pinned its ankles together and had it thrown out on the bare slopes of Kithairon. And so you see, the Oracle was proved false on both counts –'

But Oedipus was no longer listening: 'Jocasta', he broke in, 'did I hear you right? Did you say that Laius was slain where three roads meet?'

'Yes, that is what we all heard', answered Jocasta in surprise. 'The place is called Schiste: there the roads from Thebes, Daulis and Delphi meet in a narrow mountain pass.'

'When exactly did he die? And what did he look like?' asked Oedipus.

'It was shortly before you came to Thebes , answered Jocasta, 'and Laius was not unlike you, though older – a tall man, with the silver beginning to show in his hair.'

'Then it seems that I have pronounced a curse upon myself and doomed myself to exile', said Oedipus. 'Listen, and I will tell you of an adventure which I have kept to myself until now for very shame. My father, as you know, is Polybus of Corinth, and his wife Merope is my mother. One day at a banquet a man who had taken too much wine called me a bastard. When I told my parents they denied it angrily; but being at Delphi not long after, I asked for the truth from Apollo's Oracle. The god did not answer my question, but instead uttered a horrible prophecy – that I was fated to kill my father and marry my mother.

'On hearing this I vowed never to go near Corinth again, and set out to seek my fortune along the road to Thebes. On my way I came to the very place you speak of – to Schiste, where the three roads meet. There I met a chariot in which stood a man such as you describe, and before him went a herald who tried to push me roughly out of the way. In a sudden burst of anger I struck the herald with my staff so hard that he fell dead to the ground. As I tried then to pass the chariot and go on my way, the man in it struck me with his whip; I struck back and he too fell dead to the ground. There were one or two other servants as well, and these I struck down also in my wild rage, and left for dead.

'So you see: if this man was indeed Laius, I am his murderer, even though I am not his son. And the murderer of Laius, whoever he be, is doomed to exile. So I must leave Thebes; and I cannot go back to Corinth for fear of killing Polybus my father and marrying my mother Merope. There is only one ray of hope remaining to me: you said that a whole band of robbers killed Laius – well, I am only one man, and if you can find the one man who survived the attack, he will be able to tell us for certain how many were concerned in the killing of Laius.'

'I have already sent for him –' began Jocasta, when she was interrupted by the arrival of a stranger who declared himself to be a messenger from Corinth.

'I come with both bad news and good', he said. 'The bad – or rather the sad – news, is that Polybus is dead. The good is that you, Oedipus, by full acclaim of all the people, are now King of Corinth.'

'And how did he die', asked Oedipus eagerly.

'Why, of sickness such as attends old age', was the answer.

'Well, wife, you see how much faith we can place in Apollo and his Oracle!' cried Oedipus. 'He prophesied that I should kill my father – but Polybus has died a natural death . . . Unless, indeed you can say that he died of sorrow for my absence!'

'So you need put no more faith in any of these prophecies which have been troubling you', agreed Jocasta.

'Unless indeed I go and marry Merope my mother!' laughed Oedipus. 'She alone I fear.'

'What fear have you of Merope?' asked the messenger.

'An oracle', answered Oedipus. 'A lying oracle that I should kill my father and marry my mother.'

'Oh, you can put any such fear out of your head, and live

hereafter in peace', said the messenger. 'Polybus was not your father, nor was Merope your mother. They received you from my hands when you were a tiny baby.'

'From your hands?'

'Yes. You were cast out to die on Kithairon, with your feet pinned together.'

'That explains my swollen feet: I was called Oedipus – "swell-foot" – in consequence. But did you find me exposed on the mountain side?'

'No. Another shepherd gave you to me.'

'Who was he? Did he tell you anything about me?'

'No. Except that he served King Laius of Thebes.'

'Lady, can this be the man for whom you have sent?' asked Oedipus, turning to Jocasta.

'No! No!' she cried wildly. 'It is not worth a thought. Pay no attention.'

'But I must follow every clue –' began Oedipus. But Jocasta broke in even more wildly:

'By the gods, if you have any care for your own life and happiness, ask no more. Let me suffer alone.'

'Do not trouble yourself', said Oedipus bitterly. 'Even if I am the son of the vilest slave in Boeotia – a slave of three generations – *you* will not be proved base-born.'

'Ill-fated one! May you never come to know who you are!' cried Jocasta and turning she fled into the palace.

Scarcely had she gone when two of the guards appeared leading the old shepherd for whom Jocasta had sent. When he saw the Corinthian messenger, he seemed anxious to escape and for a long time refused to recognise him. But the Corinthian was certain that he was indeed the man; and threatened by Oedipus with torture if he did not speak, he confessed all:

'Yes, I was a slave reared in the household of King Laius. I gave a man child to this man. I was told to expose it on Kithairon but I had not the heart to do so. Therefore I gave it to this man to carry away far from Thebes to be brought up in Corinth.'

'Was it your own child?' asked Oedipus.

'No', answered the old shepherd, as if the words were being dragged out of him one by one. 'No. Queen Jocasta gave it to me herself... It – was – her – own – child...'

Then Oedipus, knowing all the truth at last, put his hands to his head crying: 'All is brought to pass as Apollo said! All is true! Now I look upon the light for the last time – I have been found accursed in birth, accursed in marriage and accursed in the shedding of blood!' And with a dreadful scream of agony, he turned and rushed into the palace.

Meanwhile Jocasta had frantically dashed in before him and flung herself on her bed. A moment later she sprang up, slammed the doors of the room together and shot the bolts, shrieking and sobbing that she was polluted and accursed who had married her own son and borne him children. Then she suddenly became silent with one choking cry – and on that instant Oedipus burst into the palace crying for a sword with which to kill himself. Not finding one, he flung himself against the locked doors of the bed-chamber so hard that he tore the bolts from their sockets and burst in.

And there he saw Jocasta hanging by the neck in a noose of twisted cords. And when he saw her, with a cry of utter misery he loosed the cords and laid her tenderly on the bed. Then crying like an animal caught in a snare he plucked the brooches from her garments and plunged them into his eyes, yelling:

'Eyes, no longer look upon such horrors as my anguish and my sins. You have looked on unnatural lives such as earth should never bear. Henceforth be dark for ever!'

With Oedipus blind, Creon at once became King of Thebes again since his two sons Eteocles and Polynices were still only children. Indeed, in obedience to Apollo's command from Delphi, Oedipus was forced to go into exile; but his elder daughter Antigone, a girl of about fifteen, insisted on going with him to lead him and beg food for him.

It chanced that Jocasta had been cut down in time, and she recovered slowly and remained ever after a broken woman, hiding herself away in the depth of the palace on the Cadmeia at Thebes.

VIII

THE SEVEN AGAINST THEBES

Creon, the brother of Queen Jocasta, reigned over Thebes for many years, until Eteocles and Polynices, the two sons of the blind and banished Oedipus were old enough to do so. When this time came they agreed to rule year by year, each leaving the country while his brother was on the throne.

Polynices was the first; and he honourably handed over the power to his brother for the next year. But when that year was ended, Eteocles refused to hand over to Polynices: he was intoxicated with power and was ready to do anything rather than surrender it.

'I'd go to the stars beyond the eastern sky, and down beneath the earth to get power – the greatest good the gods send to men!' he insisted. 'I have the sovereignty of Thebes: that is power, and I know that it's good, and I am going to keep it! It's cowardice to let the big thing go and settle for anything less.'

And he banished Polynices from Thebes, threatening him with death if he showed his face anywhere in Boeotia.

Polynices set off from Thebes determined to find friends who would help him to win back the kingdom. And he took with him the Necklace of Harmonia and her magic cloak both of which Jocasta had handed over to him as the elder son when he came of age.

For some time he was unsuccessful. But one night when he sought shelter at the palace of King Adrastus of Argos his fortune changed.

It happened that Adrastus had two daughters called Deipyle and Argeia, and was so concerned as to who was to marry them that he went to Delphi to seek guidance from Apollo. And the Oracle answered:

'Your daughters of age to be wed you must give to a Boar and a Lion!'

This caused Adrastus even more concern than before, and he returned to Argos puzzling anxiously over the god's strange demand.

But one night he was roused by the clash of swords and the angry shouts of men fighting, and on rushing out into the courtyard with his own weapon drawn in his hand he found two strangers battling furiously. And one of them wore a lion-skin and had a lion painted on his shield, and the other had a boar on his and wore a boar-skin across his chest.

Adrastus quickly parted them, crying: 'Why this fury, young strangers? Why are you fighting here in the night? Cease from this senseless strife and tell me who you are – noble you must be as I can tell by your looks.'

'I am Tydeus, son of King Oeneus of Calydon', answered the man in the boar skin. 'By mischance I killed my cousin while hunting, and so come here as an exile seeking your protection. I thought this man would drive me away and so I drew and attacked him: but I have no other quarrel with him and do not even know who he is.'

'I am Polynices, son of Oedipus, and rightful King of Thebes', said the lion-man. 'I wear a lion skin and bear a lion on my shield in memory of Heracles who slew the Lion of Kithairon while he dwelt at Thebes. I come to seek your help against my brother Eteocles who has usurped the throne and threatens to kill me if I dare to enter Thebes. I beg you, King Adrastus, to send an army to force him to allow me my rights, and I will swear eternal friendship between Thebes and Argos.'

When Adrastus heard these stories he realised that here were the two men Apollo had sent to be the husbands of his daughters – the bearer of the Lion of Kithairon and the bearer of the Boar of Calydon. And so he made haste to welcome them as his guests, to promise to restore both of them to their kingdoms, and to offer them his daughters in marriage. And Tydeus married Deipyle while Polynices married Argeia.

Polynices lived happily enough in Argos for some time and had a son called Thersander. But all the while he was hankering after his lost kingdom of Thebes and kept reminding Adrastus of his promise to lead an expeditionary force against the city and punish Eteocles.

Adrastus was loathe to keep his promise on account of the divinations of his friend the seer Amphiaraus – one of the holiest men in Greece and second only to Teiresias in his ability to see into the future. He foresaw that the expedition was doomed to failure, or certainly that all the chieftains who led their men against Thebes, himself included, would be killed – except for Adrastus. And without Amphiaraus Adrastus refused to march against Thebes.

In desperation Polynices went to consult Iphis, who was a lord of Argos famed for his cunning, as to how Amphiaraus might be persuaded to join the expedition.

'You may only do it through his wife Eriphyle', answered Iphis. 'If you can persuade her, she can persuade him. And indeed she is very wise and far-sighted and both Amphiaraus and Adrastus often consult her and follow her advice on matters of policy. At one time there was a quarrel between the two which might have led to civil war: she was able to decide fairly between them, and at that time both swore to let her decide any future difference that might arise.'

After much consideration Polynices went to Eriphyle and offered her the Necklace of Harmonia to vote for war against Thebes when Adrastus and Amphiaraus asked her to decide between them. This was a bribe that no woman, not even one so wise as Eriphyle, could resist, and she cast her vote on the side of Adrastus, though she knew that by so doing she would bring about her husband's death.

But these things could not be hid from Amphiaraus the seer. Knowing well how his wife had been bribed and that she knew that she was sending him to his death, Amphiaraus told his sons Alcmeon and Amphilochus and made them swear to kill Eriphyle when they were grown up and before they themselves set out to conquer Thebes.

Once Amphiaraus had been tricked into joining the expedition Adrastus made haste to gather his forces; and when he set out it was with the army in seven groups each to attack one of the seven gates of Thebes and, because there were seven chieftains the expedition was known as the Seven against Thebes. And these heroes, famous ever afterwards, were Adrastus, Amphiaraus, Capaneus and Hippomedon, all from Argos; Parthenopaeus son of Atalanta and Melanion from Tegea in Arcadia, Polynices of Thebes and Tydeus of Calydon.

Marching from Argos they took the mountain route by Nemea

and in the long valley near where the temple now stands they ran short of water and could not find a spring until Hypsipyle showed them where to look. She was the Queen of Lemnos who had been sold into slavery by the women of that island. For it chanced that the women of Lemnos incurred the wrath of Aphrodite who punished them by inflicting them with a smell so unpleasant that their husbands would have nothing to do with them, but took captive some of the wild women of Thrace instead. In revenge the Lemnian women agreed to murder all the men on the island, and all kept their oath except Hysipyle who smuggled away her father Thoas in a floating chest. And when they discovered what she had done, they sold Hypsipyle as a slave to Lycurgus, King of Nemea who made her nurse to his baby son Opheltes.

In answer to Adrastus's request for water Hypsipyle replied:

'There is a shady fountain not far away, but a serpent watches over it – a serpent with fierce red eyes and a yellow crest. The shepherds dread it, and they can only use the fountain when the serpent is away hunting for its food. I will lead you to it, for the serpent will be hunting now, or sleeping in the heat of the day.'

So saying, she laid down the boy Opheltes under a bush and led Adrastus and his men to the fountain, where the army was soon encamped, Adrastus swearing that they would kill the serpent as soon as they saw it.

But when Hypsipyle returned to where she had left Opheltes she found to her horror that the serpent had killed him. Adrastus and Amphiaraus soon killed the serpent: but this would not bring Opheltes back to life – and she herself was in danger of being killed by King Lycurgus for neglecting her charge.

Amphiaraus, however, was able to persuade Lycurgus and his wife Eurydice that Hypsipyle was innocent. And he went on:

'Give us the body of your son and we will bury him in a grave of everlasting remembrance. This sorrow of yours if not yours alone, nor shall it end when you die. This tomb shall be memorable in the eyes of all men, and we shall found the Nemean Games in his honour, and the victor's crown shall be of leaves from the bush under which your son was laid – and the winner shall be envied throughout Hellas and all men shall look up to him. But this woman Hypsipyle must go free, for indeed she is innocent. Moreover she has brought deathless honour to your house by being the innocent cause of one death. And before long her two sons shall find her here and take her with them to an honourable old age.'

All fell out as Amphiaraus prophesied, and the Argive army camped for many days in the valley and celebrated the first Nemean Games.

Before moving on it was decided to send an envoy to Thebes to see if Eteocles might give up the throne when he knew that an invading army was nearing his borders. Tydeus, the greatest warrior in the army, was chosen for this mission, and he went fearlessly to Thebes and was entertained by Eteocles in the Cadmeia. Eteocles, however, showed no inclination to give up the throne to Polynices, even for a year. Nor did Tydeus succeed in changing his mind by challenging the bravest and strongest Thebans to various contests and defeating them all.

So he set out for Nemea after twelve days in Thebes. But Eteocles could not readily forgive the defeat of all his champions and – since one bad deed begets another – he had little hesitation in sending a band of young warriors to waylay and kill Tydeus.

They lay in ambush on the lower slopes of Kithairon. Night was just falling when Tydeus saw the shimmer of shields in the undergrowth and the sunset gleaming on the points of spears.

'Where are you from? Who are you waiting for?' he called out.

He was answered with a rain of spears which he turned on his great shield. And he threw their spears back with such unerring aim that several Thebans fell dead or mortally wounded.

Then he drew his sword and charged. And he fought so mightily that all fell before him, and he spared only one to carry the news back to Thebes. This was Maeon, the son of Haemon, the eldest son of Creon, who had been one of the victims of the terrible Sphinx before Oedipus came to read her riddle.

To him Tydeus gave a message for Eteocles: 'Raise a mound before your gates, renew your weapons, see to your mouldering old walls, and start drilling your soldiers for *real* war. You have seen what I alone can do against you: think what the whole might of Argos can accomplish.'

Tydeus returned safely to the Argive army encampment at Nemea, and he brought with him one thing of great value: a prophecy which Teiresias had uttered while he was in the Cadmeia.

'Thebes will never fall if the grave of Oedipus lies within its borders. But if he is laid to rest in some foreign land, that land shall conquer Thebes.'

All these years Oedipus had been wandering about Greece as a blind beggar, led by his faithful daughter Antigone. At this time he had come into Athenian territory and, promised protection by the good King Theseus, was living quietly at Colonus on the outskirts of Athens.

On hearing of the prophecy, Polynices hastened to Colonus; but old Creon, who had immediately set out from Thebes, arrived first and found Oedipus at Colonus with Antigone still in attendance on him.

However even Creon had been forestalled by Ismene the second daughter of Oedipus, who had remained at Thebes to guard his interests and keep him in touch with all that was happening. She found him first and told him all about the prophecy so that he was ready to answer Creon and mock his sudden wish to look after him.

'You let me leave Thebes as a beggar', said Oedipus, 'and you have let me wander for all these years not knowing where my next meal was to come from, without a thought for me. But now, because you think my bones may bring you luck, you start showing concern for my condition. No: if my bones can bring luck to anyone, let it be to Theseus and the Athenians, who alone of all people have welcomed and protected me.'

At this Creon made the even worse mistake of trying to take Oedipus by force. But the Athenians under Theseus rallied round him and drove off the Thebans. After which Oedipus laid his curse on Eteocles and his followers – a curse which he extended to include Polynices who arrived soon after and protested the same sudden concern over his well-being.

'You and your brother allowed me to be driven out of Thebes as a blind and helpless beggar', said Oedipus, 'and never, either then or during the years since then, raised a hand to help me in any way. I know why you are now so suddenly anxious about my well-being, and I join you in the curse which I have just pronounced on your brother. May you divide your inheritance with your swords.'

Polynices returned to Nemea discomfited; and not long after Oedipus died or disappeared mysteriously at Colonus, leaving his blessing on Athens and the promise that Theseus should triumph over Thebes if the two cities ever came to blows.

Antigone and Ismene returned to Thebes and arrived in the city just before Adrastus and his army reached it and laid siege to it, having easily defeated the forces sent against them.

At this stage it seemed that a peaceful settlement might still be possible, and Jocasta sent a message to Polynices, with a safe-conduct, begging him to visit her.

Polynices came; and Eteocles consented to meet him, with Jocasta to try to make peace between them. But neither would yield an inch. Polynices reaffirmed his case:

'He and no other drove me from my native land and broke the bargain whereby we were to reign here in Thebes year and year about. Only because he would not yield to my certain right have I found me friends at Argos and come against my home with foreign arms.'

And Eteocles reiterated that what he had got he would hold: only a fool and a coward would give up a kingdom – and anyhow Polynices was now a traitor of the worst sort for leading an enemy army against Thebes, and no fate was bad enough for him. 'When you lie dead', he ended, 'I'll see to it that your body is left unburied for the dogs and vultures to tear to pieces – and Creon shall vow to do this if I too fall in the battle.'

So the two brothers parted, vowing to meet in battle and kill one another, and both began to prepare for the great attack on Thebes.

It seemed that Thebes was certain to fall, and in great anxiety Creon sent for Teiresias the blind prophet to ask if any sacrifice to the gods could help them.

'I would not have spoken had you not demanded an answer', said Teiresias sadly. 'But now I must speak. I tell you, Creon, this land has been sick ever since Laius brought a curse upon it and flouted the Oracle of Apollo by having a son – Oedipus – when warned what would happen if he did. That curse had had its way with Oedipus and now it rests upon his children. Eteocles and Polynices shall divide their inheritance with the sword: death by their own hands is upon them – and the curse does not end with them, for there are still others who must suffer. And Thebes must fall – unless a sacrifice is made which you could never allow and I will not name.'

'Nevertheless, you must tell me', said Creon. 'At such a time we must stick at nothing. If you do not speak freely we will have to see what torture can do.'

'Then you shall hear what I know by my prophetic art', replied Teiresias. 'The only way to save Thebes is to sacrifice your son Menoeceus to the gods. You have asked: you cannot blame me for the answer.'

'I was not listening! I did not hear!' cried Creon desperately after a moment of horror. 'Why should this curse fall on me and my innocent son?'

'You are of the seed of the Sown Men', answered Teiresias, 'and from each line so descended Ares demands a life for his holy Dragon whom Cadmus slew. Menoeceus must be slain by Dirce's stream so that his blood falls into the Dragon's den: he is of the pure blood of the Sown Men on both sides – and your other son Haemon, named after your eldest whom the Sphinx slew, is saved by his betrothal to Antigone the daughter of Oedipus and your sister Jocasta. So you have your choice: to save your city or to save your son.'

After this Teiresias was led home by his daughter Manto, and Creon turned to Menoeceus, who had listened in silence to the prophecy.

'No one would give his own son up to death!' he said, 'Quick! You must leave Thebes immediately, before the people hear of this. Go into hiding – go to Dodona and ask the Oracle of Zeus where you should dwell: I'll give you gold to help you on your way.'

'Then go and get it while I bid farewell to your sister Jocasta and to my mother', said Menoeceus, and Creon hurried off to his own house.

But Menoeceus had no intention of fleeing from Thebes, 'My father would have me play the coward', he said to himself. 'This can be forgiven in him – but not in me. I cannot betray my fatherland though I am forced to disobey my father.'

Determined on the sacrifice, he went up on to the wall of Thebes, to the tower which overlooked the Dragon's den by the Fountain of Dirce. And there he stabbed himself with his own sword so that he fell dead from the tower and lay in his blood in the place indicated by the prophecy of Teiresias.

Scarcely was he dead when the main attack developed, the Seven each attempting to win one of the seven gates of Thebes.

First Parthenopaeus, the son of Atalanta, attacked the Neitian Gate – Parthenopaeus who carried the likeness of the Sphinx on his shield. He rushed upon the Gate waving a double-axe with which to hew it down. But Periclymenus the defender of that Gate dashed a great stone down on his helmeted head and crushed it as a snail is crushed in its shell at the blow of a hammer.

Amphiaraus made for the Proetian Gate, while Capaneus with a giant painted on his shield attacked the Electran Gate and Hippomedon with many-eyed Argus on his shield scaled the Ogygian Gate. Polynices made for the Gate of the Springs and Adrastus with the Lernean Hydra on his shield tried to take the Homoloidian Gate.

Tydeus with the Boar shield scaled the Gate of Athena Onsa and nearly took it. But Eteocles sent reinforcements just in time and Tydeus fell mortally wounded with a spear through his stomach.

The battle still hung in the balance and Capaneus cried: 'Forward, men of Argos and we'll take the town! Zeus himself cannot stop me! I defy him to try!' So saying he scrambled up the scaling-ladder, paying little heed to the shower of stones that rained down upon him. From rung to rung he struggled upward, guarding his head with his shield, until he stood upon the very wall of Thebes, about to spring down inside and open the gate to the Argive army.

But at that moment Zeus struck, hurling a thunderbolt with a great flash of lightning so that the very earth shook. Back fell Capaneus, his arms and legs spinning like Ixion on his wheel of fire, and crashed to the ground outside the wall a charred corpse, while the scaling ladder crumpled in flames behind him.

When Adrastus saw this he turned and fled from Thebes and having the swiftest horses he got safely away. But few were as fortunate. The Thebans poured out of the city and pursued them, cutting down all that they overtook.

So fell the rest of the Seven Leaders. Amphiaraus did not fall with them, but by the special will of Zeus the earth opened and swallowed up him and his chariot, and he went straight to the Underworld where he became immortal: a healing Power whose shrine may still be seen at Oropus on the north coast of Attica.

But Eteocles and Polynices met in single combat and nothing could part them. They ran at one another like wild boars, their spears levelled. But they kept well behind their shields: if either saw the other peer over the top he darted with his spear, hoping to catch him quickly with its point. Presently as they dodged and circled Eteocles slipped a little on a stone that turned under his foot. One

Jael Jordan

leg came out beside the shield – and Polynices struck and pierced clean through the calf. But doing so he laid bare his shoulder, and Eteocles struck there and his spear broke leaving its head in the wound. Leaping back he snatched up a large stone and hurled it. Polynices warded it off with his spear, but the shaft broke, leaving them equally matched once more.

Drawing their swords they dashed together like mad men, neither gaining the advantage for some time. But Eteocles knew a fine Thessalian trick. Jumping back, sword poised, he suddenly swung round on one foot and plunged his blade into his brother's stomach, right through until the point lodged in his spine. Polynices fell as if dead, and shouting with triumph Eteocles began stripping off his armour as a trophy of his victory.

But Polynices, although mortally wounded, was only shamming dead, and he still had firm hold of his sword. Suddenly he thrust it up through his brother's liver and brought Eteocles dying to the ground beside him.

Just as he fell Jocasta and Antigone came running out of the city having heard that they were engaged in mortal combat and hoping to be able to separate them.

Eteocles was just able to clasp Jocasta's hand: he could not speak, but tears fell from his eyes in token of his love as he smiled at her – and died.

But Polynices could still speak: 'Mother, we're dead. I pity you, and my sisters, and this poor corpse beside me, my friend turned enemy but still my friend. Mother, I beg you and my sisters to bury me in my own land. Persuade angry Creon to grant this much of my native soil. Close my eyes and – farewell, the darkness is creeping in round me.'

So both brothers died. And then with a sudden heart-rending cry Jocasta caught up a sword and plunged it into her throat, so that she fell dying upon her two dead sons.

IX

ANTIGONE

With Eteocles and Polynices dead, Creon was once more King of Thebes; and the death of his sister and their mother – to say nothing of the passing of Oedipus to his strange fate at Colonus – made him answerable to no one. For Laodomas and Thersander, the sons of Eteocles and Polynices, were still only small babies.

Creon's first act as King of Thebes was to accord full burial honours to Eteocles and all those who had fallen in defence of the city. His next was to forbid the burial of all those who had fallen on the Argive side – and in particular of Polynices. Foreseeing that there might still be sympathisers in the city he uttered his decree as a kind of test of the full weight of his authority – which, for the first time, was now absolute:

'Polynices shall be left unburied for the birds and dogs to tear. He came as a traitor to attack his own city, and deserves no funeral honours. Moreover anyone trying to bury him or offer his body any funeral honours shall die, even if he were my own son. I have spoken, and no one shall reverse my doom.'

But at once he found someone who was ready to defy him: Antigone, the sister of Polynices.

'He must be buried', she insisted. 'It is the divine law among all civilised men.'

'He shall not be buried', shouted Creon. 'He sinned against the the divine law by fighting against his own city – yes, by leading against her an army of foreigners. Therefore he is without the law, and he shall remain unburied.'

'The law of Zeus is higher than the commands of any earthly

being', answered Antigone. 'And that is the law which must be obeyed. Rather than break the law of Zeus I'll break your wicked law, and bury him myself.'

'Though you are my niece and betrothed to my son Haemon', stormed Creon, 'if you try to bury your brother Polynices, you shall die.'

Creon thought that this had warned off Antigone from any attempt at burying the body of Polynices: but he was wrong. She at once sought out her sister Ismene and tried to obtain her help.

But Ismene was gentle and timid; and she had spent all her life in luxury in Thebes; she was very different from Antigone who from early girlhood had been her blind father's guide in the harshness of the world outside.

In terror she refused to help Antigone and thus flout the direct orders of Creon and risk a death sentence as well:

'Think how our father and mother, and our two brothers, have perished', she urged. 'Surely enough ill has befallen the unhappy house of Laius without us hazarding our lives as well!'

'If you will not help me, leave me', said Antigone. 'Let me do and suffer alone. At least you will then escape my fate.'

And so Antigone went on her mission alone, waiting until a dust-storm had caused the guards to desert their post to speed out to the body of Polynices and cover it with a layer of dust and earth.

When the guard reported to Creon that someone had given Polynices a token burial, he stormed and raged at them.

'Uncover it, and watch more carefully', he ended. 'If this happens again, I'll hang you all!'

Very soon Antigone found that her work had been undone. And this time the guards caught her sprinkling dust from a great copper urn over the corpse, and led her triumphantly to Creon, who began questioning her at once:

'Girl, did you not know of my edict forbidding the burial of Polynices?'

'I knew it well', answered Antigone calmly. 'It was published throughout the city for all to hear – how could I help but hear it?'

'And you dared to break the law I had made?'

'Yes. For Zeus has made an earlier and a greater law: not a law of yesterday or today, but for all time. By that law we must honour

Jael Jordan

the dead; and by that law my greatest duty is to perform my brother's funeral rites as his next of kin – seeing that his son is only a child and far away in Argos, and that you his uncle have not undertaken it.'

'Did you not know that by my law the doer of this deed must be put to death?' demanded Creon.

'I knew it well,' answered Antigone steadfastly. 'We must all die; and if I am to do so before my time, I count it a gain; for when anyone lives as I do, surrounded with evils, death can come as a merciful release.'

'You differ from all the rest of Thebes if you think the traitor Polynices should be buried', blustered Creon.

'Most of them think as I do – but dare not speak for fear of you', answered Antigone.

Meanwhile Ismene had repented of her refusal to help Antigone, and came to die with her even though she had not actually been guilty of breaking Creon's edict. But Creon was already sorry for what he had done: he refused to include Ismene in the sentence, but he could not spare Antigone for fear of showing weakness – and Creon was fast becoming a tyrannical dictator, who must preserve his power at all costs.

When he heard what was happening Creon's son Haemon, who was to marry Antigone and was deeply in love with her, tried to reason with his father.

'The citizens are saying that no woman ever merited her doom less', he urged. 'They are saying that her deeds are glorious and deserve golden honours – not death. I tell you this not merely because I want to save Antigone, but for your own good. The tree that stands stiffly against the tempest is apt to fall: the sapling which bends before it lives to stand upright again when the storm has passed. The sign of a really strong man is to be able to admit that he has made a mistake.'

But Creon would not listen to reason, and they argued violently ending with Haemon bursting out:

'If she dies her death will destroy another.' Creon took this as a threat to his life and power, and threatened to have Antigone executed there and then before his very eyes. This was more than Haemon could endure and he rushed away while Creon issued his cold-blooded orders to his guards:

'Take her to the lonely cave beneath the Rock of the Sphinx and wall her up in it. Leave some food with her so that we cannot be said to have contradicted the rules of piety and brought a curse on the city. And there, if she prays hard enough to Hades god of the dead – the only god whom she seems to worship – perhaps he will release her from death. If not, she will learn at last, though too late, that it is lost labour to revere the dead and disobey the living.'

Antigone was led away to her cruel doom and Creon was just beginning to feel that he had triumphed in the first real test of his power, when the blind prophet Teiresias appeared before him, led by his daughter Manto.

'Take warning, King of Thebes!' he cried. 'You are bringing a new curse upon the city. All men are liable to err: admit your error before it is too late. Allow their rites to the dead: do not seek to wound the fallen. I have always sought your good and for your good I am now speaking.'

At first Creon turned fiercely on Teiresias, accusing him of taking bribes from those who sympathised with Antigone.

But Teiresias rejected the suggestion with scorn, went on to accuse Creon of acting like a tyrant, and warned him:

'Know well that before this sun sets one close in blood to you shall lie before you dead – because you have ruthlessly lodged a living soul in the grave, and because you have kept in the light of day one who belongs by rights to the Underworld. You do violence to the gods by taking to yourself powers that are not yours to wield. Beware of the avenging destroyers, the Furies of Hades, who may soon be dogging your steps . . . Daughter, lead me home, and leave this madman to insult younger men than I and to find out by bitter suffering what it is to flout the gods and insult their prophet.'

When he was alone, Creon was suddenly overtaken by fear. What if he had incurred the vengeance of the gods? Teiresias had never been known to prophesy falsely . . . With a desperate fear gnawing at his heart, Creon began trying to undo what he had done.

First of all he led a party to the battle field where the corpse of Polynices still lay decaying in the sun, caused it to be sprinkled with scented water and laid on a pyre of pine wood where it was soon consumed to ashes. Then he set out for the cave beneath the Rock of the Sphinx to free Antigone.

As he drew near he saw that some of the stones with which the cave mouth had been built up were wrenched away, and he heard a bitter cry which struck cold to his heart, for he recognised Haemon's voice.

Rushing forward he peered into the gloom and saw Antigone hanging by the neck in a noose made by tearing her cloak into strips: she had chosen a quick death rather than the lingering agony of starvation.

Next he saw that Haemon was there bewailing the loss of his bride as he cut down the body and smothered the cold face with kisses.

Creon climbed through the broken wall, crying: 'Come out, my son, I beg and implore you! Why are you here? What rash thing are you doing?'

But Haemon turned upon him and spat in his face, and without a word drew his sword and made as if to strike him with it. Creon retreated hastily; and with a wild cry of agony Haemon set the hilt of the sword to the ground and flung himself onto the point. And before the end overtook him he had just time to clasp Antigone in his arms, united with her in death.

Sorrowfully Creon caused the bodies to be carried back to the Cadmeia. And there his wife Eurydice, who had lost her two sons in two days, stabbed herself to death.

Creon's heart may have been near to breaking at his own double loss, but it was not softened by his calamities. In obedience to Teiresias he had given Polynices full funeral honours – for Polynices was a Theban, even if he had made war against his own city, and it was understandable that if left unburied he might bring pollution and a curse upon Thebes. But the rest of the fallen Seven, and others from the army of Adrastus, were Argives and could bring no curse. So Creon reiterated his command that no funeral honours were to be paid them, and refused to yield up the bodies when heralds came under a flag of truce from Adrastus.

Having lost the war, Adrastus could not take the bodies by force. And so he looked about for someone to help him, and turned to Theseus, the noble and righteous King of Athens for assistance. With the widows of the fallen men, he made his way to Eleusis, six miles from Athens. Here they knelt at the altar in front of the Temple of Demeter, carrying the olive boughs which showed that they were suppliants.

Very soon Theseus heard about them and came in person to find out why they were there. Adrastus had scarcely told his story when a herald from Creon strode into the courtyard crying:

'Which of you is the dictator of Athens? I have a message for him from Creon, dictator of Thebes.'

'We have no dictator in Athens', answered Theseus proudly. 'All the people here are ruled by the free vote of the people themselves. I am the King, but I cannot act in any great matter without first consulting my people in their Assembly.'

'We do things better in Thebes', scoffed the herald. 'There we have one man to rule us, and not an unruly mob. And that man, Creon, sends me to say (and I and all the Theban people agree, without any nonsense of assemblies) that you must not receive Adrastus into your land nor help him in any way. His dead must not be moved by force: if you try it, there will be war between Thebes and Athens. And they do not merit burial: the thunderbolt of Zeus which slew Capaneus proves that the curse of the gods is on them. So do not be foolish: true bravery consists in saving your own skin.'

'You miserable wretch –' began Adrastus angrily.

But Theseus broke in. 'Be silent, Adrastus, and let me speak. Herald, since when has Creon been my master and able to tell me what to do or not to do? And what makes him think that he is stronger than I – Thebes than Athens? I did not begin this war: I was not with the Seven when they attacked Thebes: I merely think it right to bury the dead. I mean no harm to your city, and hope we may not even come to blows. I merely uphold the law which is common to all true Greeks: what is wrong with that? Granted the Argives did you wrong, but they are dead. You defeated them honourably, to their disgrace, and now the quarrel is ended. Come! Let the dead be burnt honourably or buried under the ground. Do you think to hurt Argos by leaving her dead unburied? It is not Argos but all Greece that you insult. If you will not let us bear away the dead – and we will carry out their obsequies beyond the Theban borders – my course is clear. I shall compel their burial. Never shall it be said that I and my city refused suppliants who came to beg me to carry out the common law of all true Hellenes.'

'You will never take the Argive dead out of my country!' shouted the herald.

'On the contrary', answered Theseus, 'I shall give them honourable burial in Athenian soil.'

'Then it is a plain declaration of war', said the herald, and set out to warn Creon.

Theseus at once gathered an army and marched over the Kithairon pass by Eleutherai and down onto the Plain of Thebes. A great battle took place outside the city in which Theseus was victorious. He could have taken and sacked Thebes, but he held his hand.

'I did not come to conquer Thebes', he said, 'but only to carry away the dead heroes who fell in the war of the Seven.'

And, no one now trying to stop him, he conveyed the bodies over the border and buried most of them on the stony ridge near Eleutherai. But the bodies of Tydeus, Parthenopaeus, Capaneus and Hippomedon he brought to Eleusis to hold grand funeral celebrations over them. Of the rest of the Seven, Polynices had already been buried by Creon, Amphiaraus had disappeared in his chariot beneath the earth – and Adrastus alone had escaped death.

When the remains of the dead were set on their funeral pyre and the wood was blazing up, Evadne the wife of Capaneus flung herself onto her husband's body and was united with him in death.

And when all was over, Adrastus swore eternal friendship between Argos and Athens, and set off for home with the suppliants who had accompanied him to Eleusis, carrying the urns which held the ashes of the dead heroes.

X

THE NECKLACE OF HARMONIA

As soon as they were old enough the sons of the 'Seven against Thebes' decided to form a new expedition against the city, to set Thersander the son of Polynices on the throne in place of Laodamas, son of Eteocles, to whom old Creon was forced to relinquish the sceptre as soon as he came of age.

Besides Thersander, these consisted of Alcmaeon and Amphilichus, the sons of Amphiaraus; Aegialeus, the son of Adrastus; Diomedes, the son of Tydeus; Promachus of Tegea, the son of Parthenopaeus; Sthenelus, the son of Capaneus and Evadne; and Polydorus, the son of Hippomedon.

When Thersander consulted the Oracle at Delphi he was told that his expedition would only be successful if Alcmaeon was its leader. Alcmaeon was loathe to go since he was still troubled about his promise to his father that he would kill his mother Eripyle who had been bribed with the Necklace of Harmonia to persuade Amphiaraus to go to his death in the first attack on Thebes. In fact she was even more deserving of death than they knew, for as soon as he heard the words of the Oracle, Thersander had made haste to bribe her with the Cloak which Athena had given to Harmonia, to persuade her sons to join the second expedition.

But when he had accepted command of the expeditionary force, which was called the Epigoni – the Afterborn –, he too went to Delphi to ask for Apollo's guidance, and the Oracle told him to attack Thebes first, and when he had won the war to kill Eripyle who had indeed been bribed by the Necklace to send Amphiaraus to his death, and had also been bribed by the Cloak to send him and his brother to the war – whether it meant their death or not.

The army of the Epigoni marched over the Kithairon pass by Eleutherai and into Boeotia where, instead of beseiging Thebes, they began laying waste the small towns and villages. But soon the Thebans under Laodamas marched out in full force and drew up their lines outside the village of Glisas near Teumessos some ten miles to the east of Thebes.

There a great battle was fought in which Aegialeus the son of Adrastus was killed, but none others of the Epigoni who achieved a smashing victory. Laodamas and all those who favoured his cause fled north to Illyria, while Alcmaeon marched to Thebes, took the city without further fighting, and handed it over to Thersander.

Teiresias the blind prophet fled north with Laodamas; but very soon death at last overtook him after seeing seven generations of Theban kings; for after a long, hot day's marching he stopped to drink of the ice-cold water of the spring called Tilphussa near Coroneia and died, and was buried there.

But his daughter Manto, who was also a prophet, did not manage to escape from Thebes. Alcmaeon captured her and dedicated her to the service of Apollo at Delphi in fulfilment of a vow he had made to offer to the god the choicest of the spoils of Thebes. She spent the rest of her life at Delphi, becoming even more famous for her prophecies than Teiresias had been – and as she seemed often inspired her name was changed to Sibylla, from 'Sibyllainein' which means to be inspired in one's tongue.

After having received further definite instructions from Apollo, Alcmaeon returned to Argos and with the help of his brother Amphilochus he killed Eripyle. As she had no other son to avenge her, the Furies were sent from Hell to torment Alcmaeon and drive him mad with remorse and a haunting sense of blood-guilt.

Pursued by the Furies, Alcmaeon fled from Argos and went first to his grandfather Oicles in Arcadia. But receiving no help from him he went further west to Psophis where King Phegeus was able to purify him from his blood-guilt. And for a time Alcmaeon settled down there and married Arsinoe the daughter of Phegeus: and he gave her the Necklace of Harmonia.

But soon the ground about Psophis grew barren; the corn withered or did not come up at all, the grass turned brown in early spring, and the grapes on the vines never swelled but remained like little hard raisins.

Jael Jordan

Phageus sent messengers to Delphi to consult the Oracle; and the answer came back:

'Wherever Alcmaeon dwells the earth will turn barren. Let him find a land which did not exist when he killed his mother – for there only can he find complete purification.'

In despair Alcmaeon set out alone from Psophis and wandered about Greece trying to solve the meaning of the Oracle.

At last he came to Calydon to the north of the western end of the Gulf of Corinth, and there King Oeneus was able to help him. As they stood on the citadel of Calydon, Oeneus pointed down towards the flat marshy country where the River Achelous meanders out into the sea amid mud-flats and stagnant salt lagoons.

'The sea and the river between them seem ever to be casting up new lands and flooding old ones', he said. 'Surely there, if anywhere, you will find a patch of earth that was not there when you committed the murder from which you are seeking to be purified.'

Cheered by this suggestion, Alcmaeon set out for the Achelous and found a fine stretch of land on which it was quite obvious that the sun had not shone for long. Here he settled, and was quickly joined by other wanderers and by local families of farmers and fishermen. And before long he was freed from the curse that followed him and fully cleansed of the blood-guilt by Achelous the God of the River himself.

So he married Callirrhoe, the River-God's daughter, and made his home on the citadel of Oeniadai rising up like a steep, rocky island out of the fertile mud-flats which became his kingdom.

At first he and Callirrhoe lived happily together and had two sons called Amphoterus and Acarnan. But fearing that her beauty might fade and he desert her, she persuaded him to return to Psophis and get the Necklace of Harmonia for her: for whoever wore the Necklace retained her beauty until the end of her life.

Alcmaeon was loathe to revisit Psophis and his deserted wife Arsinoe, but Callirrhoe refused to have anything to do with him until he brought her the Necklace. And so he set out with only a few followers, crossed the Gulf of Corinth and soon came to Psophis. Here he told Phegeus that he was still being pursued by the Furies, and that Apollo had told him that he could have no rest until the Necklace of Harmonia was deposited in his temple at Delphi.

His story was believed, more particularly by Arsinoe who was tired of living as a widow at Psophis, and had no idea that Alcmaeon had another wife at Oeniadai. So she willingly gave up the Necklace, and Harmonia's Cloak also, and Alcmaeon prepared to set off with them as if for Delphi.

But one of his servants had been gossiping with a servant of Phegeus, and this servant told his master all about Callirrhoe and the real destination of the Necklace and the Cloak. In great anger Phegeus summoned his two sons Promachus and Echephron, told them the whole story and bade them kill Alcmaeon. So they lay in ambush for him, knowing from his servant that he would come below Arsinoe's window before he left for Delphi. And when he appeared they sprang out and killed him before he had a chance to defend himself.

Arsinoe was watching from her window, and she shrieked aloud when she saw the deed they were doing. In vain they tried to tell her how richly Alcmaeon deserved his fate. She stopped her ears and cursed them and her father for making her a widow indeed and for transgressing against the sacred duty of a host to protect his guest.

'May you die a violent death, all three of you!' she screamed. 'Father Zeus, hear me! Bring them to their end by violence before this moon wanes and waxes again!'

Hoping to avert the curse, Phegeus shut up Arsinoe in a chest and sent her to King Agapenor of Nemea as a slave. But to his sons he said:

'Take the Necklace of Harmonia, and the Cloak too, and dedicate them to Apollo at Delphi. He will see to it that they cause no further mischief. And maybe he will avert your sister's curse.'

They set out at once. But already Alcmaeon's servants were speeding back to Oeniadai with the news of his murder.

When Callirrhoe heard of it she prayed to Zeus for help, saying:

'Great Zeus, avenge me! Let my infant sons grow up quickly and kill Phegeus and his sons!'

Zeus heard her prayer and granted it in a way that she could hardly have expected. On a sudden the two baby boys Amphoterus and Acarnan became full grown men and at once set out for Delphi. Finding that they were too late, they followed the two sons of Phegeus back to Nemea where they had stopped to see if they could persuade Arsinoe to release them from the curse. They tried to tell her the truth about Alcmaeon, but still she would not listen. And there Amphoterus and Acarnan overtook them and killed them both.

Then the two avengers hastened on to Psophis and killed Phegeus before the next full moon. And they buried Alcmaeon at Psophis in a grave surrounded by cypress trees which grew so tall that they cast their shadows on the mountains on either side of the valley. The inhabitants of Psophis called them 'the Maidens' and would never cut any of them down, holding them sacred to Alcmaeon.

As for the fatal Necklace of Harmonia, it remained safely in the Temple of Apollo at Delphi for many hundreds of years until in the time of Philip of Macedon, Alexander the Great's father, Phayllus the tyrant of Phocis sacked Delphi and took the Necklace for his paramour the wife of Ariston of Oeata. She wore it for some time and was much admired. But before long the curse fell on her family: her youngest son went mad and set fire to the palace – and both she and the Necklace were destroyed in the flames. But some say that the Necklace survived the fire and was still to be seen five hundred years later in the Temple of Aphrodite at Amathus in Cyprus.

Meanwhile Thersander reigned peacefully over Thebes. And very soon he and the rest of the Epigoni led their armies to fight at the Siege of Troy, in which Diomedes the son of Tydeus became one of the most famous heroes.

But that is a tale that has often been told in song and in story.